T0114475

THE PSYCHOLOGY OF GRIEF

What is happening emotionally when we grieve for a loved one? Is there a 'right' way to grieve? What effect does grief have on how we see ourselves?

The Psychology of Grief is a humane and intelligent account that highlights the wide range of responses we have to losing a loved one and explores how psychologists have sought to explain this experience. From Freud's pioneering psychoanalysis to discredited ideas that we must pass through 'stages' of grief, the book examines the social and cultural norms that frame or limit our understanding of the grieving process, as well as looking at the language we use to describe it.

Everyone, at some point in their lives, experiences bereavement and *The Psychology of Grief* will help readers understand both their own and others' feelings of grief that accompany it.

Richard Gross works for Cruse Bereavement Care, the UK's largest organisation offering bereavement support. He has been an author of books in psychology for over 30 years.

THE PSYCHOLOGY OF EVERYTHING

The Psychology of Everything is a series of books which debunk the myths and pseudo-science surrounding some of life's biggest questions.

The series explores the hidden psychological factors that drive us, from our sub-conscious desires and aversions, to the innate social instincts handed to us across the generations. Accessible, informative, and always intriguing, each book is written by an expert in the field, examining how research-based knowledge compares with popular wisdom, and illustrating the potential of psychology to enrich our understanding of humanity and modern life.

Applying a psychological lens to an array of topics and contemporary concerns – from sex to addiction to conspiracy theories – *The Psychology of Everything* will make you look at everything in a new way.

Titles in the series:

For further information about this series please visit www.thepsychologyofeverything.co.uk

THE PSYCHOLOGY OF GRIEF

RICHARD GROSS

Routledge
Taylor & Francis Group

LONDON AND NEW YORK

First published 2018
by Routledge
2 Park Square, Milton Park, Abingdon, Oxon OX14 4RN

and by Routledge
605 Third Avenue, New York, NY 10017

Routledge is an imprint of the Taylor & Francis Group, an informa business

Copyright © 2018 Richard Gross

The right of Richard Gross to be identified as author of this work
has been asserted by him in accordance with sections 77 and 78 of
the Copyright, Designs and Patents Act 1988.

All rights reserved. No part of this book may be reprinted or
reproduced or utilised in any form or by any electronic, mechanical,
or other means, now known or hereafter invented, including
photocopying and recording, or in any information storage or
retrieval system, without permission in writing from the publishers.

Trademark notice: Product or corporate names may be trademarks or
registered trademarks, and are used only for identification and
explanation without intent to infringe.

British Library Cataloguing-in-Publication Data
A catalogue record for this book is available from the British Library

Library of Congress Cataloging-in-Publication Data
A catalog record for this book has been requested

ISBN: 978-1-138-08806-1 (hbk)
ISBN: 978-1-138-08807-8 (pbk)

Typeset in Joanna
by Apex CoVantage, LLC

CONTENTS

1

LOSS, BEREAVEMENT, AND GRIEF
WHAT DO THEY MEAN?

INTRODUCTION

It was while running the basic training course for Cruse Bereavement Care a few years ago that the idea of writing a book on grief first occurred to me. That course explores the nature of grief, how it's experienced, the different forms it can take, and beliefs and attitudes regarding what's 'normal' or 'healthy' grief. It also considers social and cultural attitudes to death and grief, as well as major theories of grief, which attempt to describe and explain why grief occurs and what its purpose is.

One major limitation of theories is that they involve *generalisations*, that is, they're meant to apply to everyone equally. But it soon became evident to me when working with bereaved people that everyone's grief is unique to them: generalisations may provide a framework, but real people don't fit neatly into theoretical boxes and patterns.

From my own experience of 'losing' people close to me, I would suggest that part of the uniqueness of everyone's grief is that we never know how another's death will affect us until it happens! What (certain) theories predict will be our likely reaction, and the reality of that reaction, are often worlds apart: it may not be until a person's death that we begin to appreciate the true nature of our relationship with him or her. We might grieve for the relationship we *thought* we had, or the one we *wished* we'd had, rather than the one we *actually* had. Just as relationships are complex, so can be grief.

In this and the following six chapters, I try to sample both personal experiences and theoretical accounts of grief; they are both valid in their different ways. But I think that before you begin reading, you should accept the guiding principle that there's no single 'correct' way to grieve, which includes not being able to put a time limit on the grieving process: sometimes, grief may continue for a lifetime, because we continue to love the person we have lost. While death and taxes have famously been cited as the only certainties in life, we could add grief to that list. The link between death and grief is love (sometimes 'attachment'): we grieve for those we loved who have died.

'I'M SORRY FOR YOUR LOSS'

'I'm sorry for your loss' has become a familiar and an almost clichéd acknowledgement in Western countries (especially the U.S. and U.K.) of the death of someone who was emotionally significant to the person being addressed. If we try to 'unpack' the statement, we'll identify a number of key terms – and assumptions – that recur throughout this book. (You might like to have a go at doing this yourself.)

> I recognise that X has died (is *deceased*) and I know that s/he was an important person in your life. *Bereavement* is probably the most difficult experience that any of us has to go through in our lives and you will inevitably go through a process of *grieving* for X. This is going to be tough, but it's a necessary part of your attempt to come to terms with X's death in order to be able to move on with your life.

So, what has this 'unpacking' revealed?

Bereavement refers to the loss, through death, of someone to whom we were very close emotionally ('attached') or who, in some other way, played an important part in our lives ('loved one' or 'significant other'). Grief refers to the way we respond to bereavement. As we shall see, it can take many different forms, but we assume that, in some form or another, grief is *inevitable*. Grief is commonly defined as a *universal* reaction to bereavement (i.e. observed in all cultures and throughout human history), involving bodily/physical, emotional, cognitive, and spiritual experiences and expressed in a wide range of observable behaviours. These experiences and behaviours are described in detail in Chapter 2.

Not only is grief inevitable, but we *need* to grieve: this is our way ('nature's way'?) of helping us come to terms and accept that our loved one has died. Together, the inevitability and necessity of grief point to the concept of 'grief work' (i.e. the process by which we detach ourselves emotionally from the deceased in order to form new attachments/relationships and get on with the rest of our lives).

PRIMARY AND SECONDARY LOSS

In the above 'unpacking' example, 'loss' is being used *metaphorically* (i.e. in a non-literal way): when someone dies, we haven't 'lost' them in the way we may lose (usually, more accurately, 'mislay') our keys or mobile phone (in fact, we don't usually play any part – active or passive – in their death). Using 'loss' for 'death' is not just metaphorical but also *euphemistic*: while 'dead' is 'forever', 'lost' at least implies the possibility of 'being found'. In other words, 'loss' is much 'softer', much 'kinder' than 'death', a gentler, more 'caring' way of acknowledging what's actually happened.

The loss in 'I'm sorry for your loss' is also *primary*: it refers to *who* has died and involves both a *physical* loss (the deceased person is no longer physically, literally 'there') and a *relational* loss (the breaking of the relationship or attachment [emotional tie] with that person).[1] Importantly, this display of sympathy makes no acknowledgement – even unconsciously/implicitly – of the (often multiple) *secondary* losses brought about by the primary loss. These refer to *what* has been lost: the consequences or fall-out of the loved one's death. For example, losing a husband or wife instantly deprives you of the status of 'married person': you become a widow/widower, a new, undesirable identity by which society (re-)defines you. Less explicitly and 'officially' is the changed identity that comes with the death of your second parent: many older adults bereaved in this way describe themselves as having become an orphan. (The effects of the death of different relatives – or 'kinship' – are discussed in Chapter 5.)

Traditionally at least, a widow may lose the financial security she enjoyed while married; again traditionally, widowers may find themselves deprived of the person who performed various practical tasks for them (such as cooking and washing). These and other consequences of bereavement are essentially *practical*: they relate to tangible features of everyday life, which, in principle, someone else can easily take over. But they also have *psychological* significance: they derive their *meaning* through forming part of the ongoing relationship between the partners.

Even more psychologically and emotionally relevant are the *symbolic* consequences: the loss of one's dreams, hopes, or faith.[2] Implicitly, and/or explicitly, every attachment is *future-orientated*: there are shared hopes and expectations regarding what lies ahead for the relationship. The death of one of them immediately and fundamentally shatters these hopes and plans.

Such shattering of dreams is seen even more poignantly when the primary loss involves the loss of a child. Most people, in Western countries at least, consider the death of a child as the most 'agonising and distressing source of grief'.[3] Again:

> The loss of a child will always be painful, for it is in some way a loss of part of the self. . . . In any society, the death of a young child seems to represent some failure of family or society and some loss of hope.[4]

Whether the death occurs pre-natally, at the time of birth, or when the child is still a baby, the parents' hopes and dreams for the life of their child will be destroyed. This applies also with older children or adolescents/young adults. In all cases, the future itself seems to have been destroyed (again, see Chapter 5).

Questioning one's religious faith – and perhaps even abandoning it (at least temporarily) – may be another major secondary loss ('How could there be a God if He allowed this to happen?'). It's precisely at times like this that people's faith would normally serve as a great source of comfort, so for a bereaved person to question it demonstrates the impact that grief can have.

One theory of grief that puts secondary losses at the heart of the experience of grief is *psychosocial transition theory* (PSTT).[5] When a loved one dies, everything that we previously took for granted about our lives (our *assumptive world* or 'normality') is shattered: we have to construct a 'new normal' in which the deceased plays no part. (PSTT is one of several theories of grief discussed in Chapter 3.)

ARE THERE DIFFERENT KINDS OF GRIEF?

How others perceive and relate to widowed individuals can affect the bereaved person's self-perception (their identity). If the new social status is a more negative one, then the new identity will also be more negative. This is just one example of how bereavement is a *social* phenomenon: it always, inevitably, takes place within a particular social context. If grief represents the individual's attempt to come to terms with his/her bereavement, then this is likely to be influenced by widely-shared beliefs and expectations regarding (a) its expression and (b) its duration. Regarding (a), 'common sense' understanding of grief regards it as 'normal' that bereaved people will be at the very least noticeably upset, and as regards (b) this overt grief (as well as the more private, inner grief) will last for, say, 12 months (up to the first anniversary of the death). Bereaved people are often told (at various intervals, often before the first anniversary) that they should be 'over it by now'.

What this means is that if someone fails to display any obvious signs of grief, or if their overt grief lasts more than, say, 12 months, they might be judged as behaving 'abnormally' ('I'm worried about X; her grief isn't normal'). In fact, these informal, common-sense beliefs correspond to two forms of *complicated grief* that have been investigated scientifically by psychiatrists and psychologists, namely

(i) *absent* (*minimal, inhibited,* or *delayed*) grief and (ii) *chronic* grief, respectively.[6] (Complicated grief is discussed in Chapter 6.)

DISENFRANCHISED GRIEF

Another important demonstration of the impact of social norms on individuals' response to bereavement comes in the form of *disenfranchised grief*. At its simplest, disenfranchised grief (DG) is grief that's not recognised by others as 'legitimate' or 'reasonable'. It refers to a situation where a loss isn't openly acknowledged, socially sanctioned, or publicly shared.[7]

Certain *types of losses* (e.g. divorce, parental deaths, pet loss), *relationships* (e.g. lovers, ex-partners/spouses, gay/lesbian partners/spouses), *grievers* (e.g. the very old, very young, people with learning disabilities), and *circumstances of the death* (e.g. AIDS, suicide, alcohol, or drug abuse) may all be thought of as disenfranchised (see Chapter 4).

In some of these examples, individuals have to conceal their grief from others in order to conceal the relationship whose loss has triggered it. An extreme example would be where the deceased was loved 'from afar' (by someone s/he might not even have known). In all these cases, the bereaved individual would be regarded as 'having no right' to grieve in the eyes of others ('society').

DG could be thought of as comprising two components: (i) it is 'unrecognised' grief (e.g. 'it didn't occur to me that a lesbian would respond in the same way as a heterosexual partner/spouse to death of a partner'); and (ii) 'stigmatised' grief (e.g. 'if homosexual relationships are 'unnatural', then their grief cannot be 'natural' either').

INTUITIVE AND INSTRUMENTAL GRIEF

Another important distinction is that between *intuitive* and *instrumental grieving*.[8] These represent two distinct *patterns* (or *styles*) of grief and differ according to (i) the cognitive ('intellectual') and affective ('emotional') components of *internal* experience of loss; and (ii) the individual's *outward expression* of that experience.

In *intuitive grief*, more energy is converted into the *affective* domain and less into the *cognitive*. Grief consists primarily of profoundly painful feelings (including shock and disbelief, overwhelming sorrow, and sense of loss of control). Intuitive grievers tend to spontaneously express their painful feelings through crying and want to share their inner experiences with others.

By contrast, *instrumental grief* converts most energy into the *cognitive* domain; painful feelings are tempered: grief is more of an *intellectual* experience. Instrumental grievers may channel energy into *activity*

Most people adopt a *blend* of both patterns, although any one individual may display one to a greater degree than the other. The overall responses of 'blended grievers' are more likely to correlate with the *stage* or *phase* accounts of grief (see Chapter 2).[9] For example, early on, the bereaved person may need to suppress feelings in order to arrange the funeral (and is often still in a state of shock); later, s/he may give full vent to feelings, seeking help and support. Later still, cognitive-driven action may take precedence over affective expression: the griever has to go back to work, resume parenting roles, and so on.

Women are more likely to be intuitive grievers, while men are more likely to be instrumental grievers. However, this *doesn't* mean that gender *determines* (or *causes*) an individual's grieving style; rather, gender *influences* how someone will grieve.[10]

BEREAVEMENT SUPPORT

This distinction between intuitive and instrumental grief is relevant to understanding the nature and function of *bereavement support*. At the heart of bereavement support and counselling is the assumption that clients need to acknowledge and express their grief. This may be facilitated in several different ways, but the *primary* means of expression – and the major tool used by supporters and counsellors to enable the client to do this – is *language*. As Shakespeare put it:

Give sorrow words; the grief, that does not speak,
Whispers the o'er-fraught heart, and bids it break.[11]

Shakespeare might have been describing the intuitive griever, who is likely to be better at putting feelings and thoughts into words (or *externalising* them in some other way, as in art or music) than instrumental grievers: they confront their feelings directly, rather than (re-)channelling them through other activities as instrumental grievers tend to do.

> Retelling the story and re-enacting the pain is a necessary part of grieving and an integral part of the intuitive pattern of grieving. It also represents the intuitive griever's going 'with' the grief.[12]

GRIEF, GRIEF WORK, AND MOURNING

Sigmund Freud, the famous Austrian psychoanalyst, was the first to formally address the nature of grief (see Chapter 2) and its function (see Chapter 3) in *Mourning and Melancholia* in 1917.[13] 'Mourning' describes the bereaved person's attempts to redefine his/her relationship to the deceased, his/her sense of self, and the external world. 'Successful' mourning, according to Freud, involves the severing of the emotional ties to the deceased and investing emotional energy in new relationships. This emotional separation from the loved one is achieved through 'grief work' (rather than 'mourning work') and is central to a number of well-known and influential theories/models of grief (see Chapters 2 and 3).

However, 'mourning' is also used in a very different sense to denote 'the culturally patterned expressions or rituals that accompany loss and allow others to recognise that one has become bereaved'.[14] Public displays of grief include funerals, wearing black clothes or armbands, and covering mirrors in Jewish homes. People are often described as 'being in mourning' for a deceased loved one: their normal routines and activities are suspended until the period of mourning is over (see Chapter 4). It would be very odd to describe them as 'being in grieving', rather than just 'grieving', which denotes the *individual* response to bereavement (as opposed to *social* rituals and traditions).[15]

HOW DO WE KNOW WHAT WE KNOW ABOUT GRIEF?

PERSONAL ACCOUNTS

One major source of information about the nature of grief are the *personal accounts* of bereaved individuals. Many such accounts have been written by well-known authors (such as C.S. Lewis, Dannie Abse, and Julian Barnes[16]), but also include first-time authors, driven to describing their grief both as a way of coming to terms with their loss and as a form of dedication to their loved one. These accounts tell us how grief is *experienced*; arguably, these first-hand accounts capture the nature of grief more accurately than any other method (see Chapter 2).

CLINICAL STUDIES

Freud's *Mourning and Melancholia* represents a more detached, less personal account, but one which reflects a particular theoretical bias, namely psychoanalytic theory (sometimes 'psychoanalysis'). Although Freud's ideas are important in their own right, it is his influence on later theorists and researchers (including Bowlby and Parkes) that makes him such a key figure in the *clinical study* of grief (i.e. the treatment of bereaved people whose grief may be described as complicated, informing us about the nature of both this and 'normal' grief). (These later theories are discussed in Chapters 2 and 3.)

EMPIRICAL STUDIES

Probably most of what we understand about grief derives from research studies involving large numbers of bereaved people (as opposed to individuals, as in personal accounts and clinical studies). These *empirical* (i.e. scientific, evidence-based) studies are often conducted by psychiatrists, such as Parkes, in order to understand the circumstances under which bereavement can lead to psychiatric disorders and to set up programmes of treatment and prevention. Four such influential studies are the Bethlem, London, Harvard, and Love and Loss Studies.

The Bethlem Study[17] investigated reactions to bereavement among 21 people (male and female) seeking psychiatric help on average 72 weeks following the death. Interviews were conducted at the Bethlem Royal and Maudsley Hospitals (in London). The London Study[18] attempted to find out how an unselected group of widows under 65 would cope within the first year of bereavement (i.e. they weren't seeking psychiatric help). They were interviewed at the end of the first, third, sixth, ninth, and thirteenth months (allowing for the 'anniversary reaction').[19]

The Harvard Study[20] involved 68 unselected widows and widowers (aged 45 and under) at Harvard Medical School in Boston, Massachusetts. They were interviewed 14 months after bereavement and compared with a control group of 68 married men and women of the same age, social class background, and family size.[21] Finally, the Love and Loss Study[22] involved 278 psychiatric outpatients at the Royal London Hospital and was aimed at testing the hypothesis that love and loss are inseparable, that childhood attachment patterns, separations from parents, and relationships in later life all influence how we cope with stress and loss and predict the kinds of problems which cause people to seek help following bereavement in adult life. A control group of 78 young women who hadn't sought any psychiatric help was used, 35 of whom had suffered bereavement in the previous five years.

ANTHROPOLOGICAL AND ETHNOGRAPHIC STUDIES

These studies attempt to identify patterns of grief across different cultures and so are essential for testing the claim that grief is a universal reaction to bereavement. Traditionally, such studies have focused on rituals and beliefs surrounding death (in particular regarding the afterlife) – rather than the psychological (i.e. individual) aspects of grief. A widely-made distinction is that between individualistic (typically

Western industrialised/capitalist) and *collectivist* (non-Western, traditional) societies/cultures (see Chapter 4).

IS THERE A POSITIVE SIDE TO GRIEF?

Finally, bereavement is conventionally regarded as just about the worst thing that can happen to a person and, by the same token, grief is seen as an inherently negative experience – by definition, painful and unpleasant. However, research conducted within Positive Psychology has shown that trauma of various kinds – including sudden and traumatic bereavement – can serve as a catalyst for *positive* changes. This is referred to as *post-traumatic growth* (PTG) and is the subject of Chapter 7.

2

THE EXPERIENCE AND NATURE OF GRIEF
WHAT IS IT LIKE?

In Chapter 1 we defined grief as a response to the death of a loved one or significant other (the 'primary' loss). We should also note that, strictly, it's the *perception* or *belief* that someone has died which sets this process in motion: sometimes, a reported death may involve mistaken identity, but so long as we believe that it's our loved one who has died (and this, if it happens, is likely to involve a sudden and traumatic death), then we will react accordingly. Equally, the definition needs to be qualified in that the death doesn't need to have actually taken place (yet): *anticipatory grief* refers to the response to an *expected* death, even if this lies an indeterminate time in the future (as when someone is diagnosed with a terminal illness). Anecdotally at least, relatives of those with dementia often talk of the 'death' of the person they knew before s/he actually dies.

We also noted in Chapter 1 that two major sources of our knowledge and understanding of grief are (i) personal accounts and (ii) more formal theoretical accounts focusing on the *nature* of grief (as distinct from the *function* of grief, which will be discussed in Chapter 3). In this chapter, the focus will be on those formal theoretical accounts which are more accurately thought of as *descriptive* models or theories.[1]

STAGE OR PHASE ACCOUNTS OF GRIEF

Part of the 'common sense' understanding of grief is the belief that the bereaved progress through a fixed series of stages. These beliefs regarding the natural 'course' of grief reflects the theoretical accounts proposed by psychiatrists and others working in the area of death and dying, which have found their way into popular cultural understanding. The two most commonly cited are those of Bowlby (and Bowlby and Parkes)[2] and Kübler-Ross.[3]

BOWLBY'S (AND BOWLBY AND PARKES'S) FOUR PHASES OF MOURNING

Observations of how individuals respond to the loss of a close relative show that over the course of weeks and months their responses usually move through a succession of phases. Adult grief is an extension of a general distress response to separation commonly observed in young children, and so can be regarded as a form of *separation anxiety* in response to the disruption of an attachment bond (see Chapter 3).

In the *phase of numbing*, numbness and disbelief, which can last from a few hours up to a week, may be punctuated by outbursts of extremely intense distress and/or anger. This is followed by the *phase of yearning and searching* for the deceased, which can last for months and sometimes years. In the *phase of disorganisation and despair*, feelings of depression and apathy occur when old patterns have been discarded. Finally, the *phase of greater or lesser degree of reorganisation* represents recovery from grief and acceptance of what has taken place.

The relationship with the deceased continues to fill a central role in a bereaved person's emotional life, although this generally changes form over the months and years. This continuing relationship explains the yearning and searching, as well as the anger, characteristic of phase 2, and the despair and subsequent acceptance of loss as irreversible that occur when phases 3 and 4 are passed through successfully.

KÜBLER-ROSS'S FIVE STAGES OF ANTICIPATORY GRIEF

Kübler-Ross's stage account was based on her pioneering work with more than 200 terminally ill patients. She was interested in how they prepared for their imminent deaths (*anticipatory grief*), and so her stages describe the *process of dying*. However, the stages were later applied (by other researchers) to *grief for others*; her account remains very influential in nursing and counselling with both dying patients and the bereaved.

The first stage, *denial and isolation* ('No, not me, it cannot be true') prevents the patient from being overwhelmed by the initial shock and is used by most patients not only at this early stage of their illness but also later on. Denial acts as a buffer, allowing the patients time to develop other coping mechanisms. Searching for a second opinion was a very common initial response, representing a desperate attempt to change the unpredictable world they had just been catapulted into, back into the world they knew and understood.[4]

The denial and isolation stage is followed by *anger* ('Why me? It's not fair!'): this may be directed at doctors, nurses, relatives, other healthy people who will go on living, or God. This can be the most difficult stage for family and staff to deal with: they may react personally to the patient's anger and respond with anger of their own, which only increases the patient's hostile behaviour.[5]

The third stage, *bargaining* ('Please God, let me . . .') represents an attempt to postpone death by 'doing a deal' with God (or fate, or the hospital), much as a child might bargain with its parents to get its own way. It sets a self-imposed 'deadline', such as a son or daughter's wedding or the birth of a grandchild: the patient promises not to ask for more time if this postponement is granted.

Bargaining is followed by *depression* ('How can I leave all this behind?'): This is likely to arise when the patient realises that no bargain can be struck, and that death is inevitable. S/he grieves for all the losses that death represents. This is *preparatory depression*, a form of preparatory grief that helps the patient to finally separate from the world. *Reactive depression* involves expressions of fear and anxiety, and a sense of great loss (see the discussion of *secondary loss* in Chapter 1).

Finally, in *acceptance* ('Leave me be, I'm ready to die') the patient seems to have given up the struggle for life, sleeps more, and withdraws from other people, as if preparing for 'the long journey'.

AN EVALUATION OF STAGE/PHASE ACCOUNTS OF GRIEF

One of the problems with stage accounts is that they imply that individuals *should* pass through this fixed series of stages, implying, in turn, that this is the 'correct' and universal way to experience and respond to loss. However, this is merely an *assumption* held by researchers, other professionals, and the general population.

But could the belief that these stage accounts of grief stipulate a fixed order that applies rigidly to everyone itself be a myth? For example:

> Admittedly these phases are not clear cut, and one individual may oscillate for a time back and forth between any two of them. Yet an overall sequence can be discerned.[6]

Similarly, Kübler-Ross's stages can last for different periods of time and can replace each other or coexist.[7]

Both Kübler-Ross's and Bowlby's accounts were proposed before prolonged, detailed follow-up studies of bereaved people had been conducted. For example, Parkes's London Study (see Chapter 1) showed that, with the possible exception of shock and disbelief, the process of change over time is much more a mixture of reactions which wax and wane in relation to external events and may be delayed, prolonged, or exaggerated according to the individual's mental state and circumstances.[8] Consistent with this view is C.S. Lewis's description of his personal account of grief for his wife:

> For in grief, nothing 'stays put'. One keeps on emerging from a phase, but it always recurs. Round and round. Everything repeats.[9]

Again, grief is like a 'long valley, a winding valley', one in which you are likely to encounter 'the same sort of country you thought you had left behind miles ago'.[10]

A different type of criticism, specifically of Kübler-Ross's account, is made by Parkes:[11] he observes that her claim to have discovered the 'stages of grief' fails to acknowledge that they were originally described by Robertson and Bowlby[12] in their studies of children separated from their mothers and applied to adult bereavement by Bowlby and Parkes. She clearly knew about Bowlby's and Parkes's work but makes no reference to it in her 1969 book.

Some researchers prefer to talk about the *components* of grief, such as *shock, disorganisation, denial, depression, guilt, anxiety, aggression, resolution,* and *reintegration.* Some of these components occur early, others late in the grieving process.[13]

A different approach to analysing grief in terms of component responses is to identify specific examples of *physical* (somatic or bodily), *affective* (or emotional), *cognitive, spiritual,* and *behavioural* reactions.

SPECIFIC EXAMPLES OF PHYSICAL, AFFECTIVE, COGNITIVE, SPIRITUAL, AND BEHAVIOURAL GRIEF REACTIONS

Physical/somatic reactions include headaches, aching muscles, nausea, exhaustion, menstrual irregularities, loss of appetite, general pain, insomnia, tenseness, and sensitivity to noise. *Affective/emotional reactions* include sadness, anger, guilt, jealousy, fear and anxiety, shame, relief, emancipation, powerless/hopelessness, pining, and emotional pain.

A woman whose husband died almost instantly of a stroke in his mid-50s described her anger not at him, but at the fact that that he *didn't know* that he was going to die, didn't have time to say farewells to her and their children.

> This is a form of being angry with the universe. An anger at indifference – the indifference of life merely continuing until it merely ends.[14]

Cognitive reactions can take the form of obsessive thoughts, inability to concentrate, fantasising, apathy, dreams, disorientation and confusion, going over and over the circumstances of the loss, a sense of the deceased's presence (hallucinations), and attempts to rationalise or understand the loss.

Spiritual reactions involve the search for *meaning* in loss, asking about the meaning and purpose of life without the deceased, and changes in spiritual and religious feelings or beliefs.

Finally, *behavioural responses* include crying, illness-related behaviours (e.g. observable symptoms), outward expression of emotion, observable changes in spiritual behaviours/expressions, searching behaviours, avoiding or seeking reminders of the deceased, obsessive activity, activities that provide some sense of connection to the deceased (e.g. visiting the cemetery), physical activities (e.g. exercise, gardening), social withdrawal, absentmindedness, accidents, and increased use of alcohol, tobacco, and other substances.

However, any purely descriptive account of grief as a series of components might (unintentionally) imply a set of independent reactions; at least the stage approach provides a *holistic* view, i.e. recognising that these various components must be organised into some *whole*.[15] Similarly, stages provide a *framework* for understanding the experiences of the bereaved (and dying individuals). A *sequence* or *pattern* is often observed: numbness, commonly the first response, gives way to pining, which is often followed by a period of disorganisation and despair; in the long run, this too declines as acceptance grows.[16] Many people use the term 'recovery' to describe this time, although we're all, to some degree, *permanently* changed by our losses.

Clearly, each of these 'states' of grief has its own characteristics and there are considerable individual differences both in terms of their duration and form. While there's a tendency for the symptoms that distinguish these phases/stages to *peak* in the order described,[17] one phase doesn't have to end before the next can begin, and there's considerable *overlap* between them.[18] For all these reasons, 'phases' (or 'stages') of grief tend not to be used any longer: the framework they provide is too rigid.

Perhaps the greatest value of phase/stage accounts has been to draw attention to the fact that grief is a *process* that people pass through and that, in doing so, most tend to move from a state of relative disorientation and distress to one of growing understanding and acceptance of the loss.[19]

GIVING GRIEF WORDS: THE USE OF METAPHOR

As noted in Chapter 1, central to bereavement support and counselling is the belief that clients need to acknowledge and express their grief. The *primary* means of expression – and the major tool used by supporters and counsellors to enable the client to do this – is *language*. However, while it's generally agreed that we need to 'give sorrow words' (as Shakespeare advised), finding the words that accurately capture how we feel is often very difficult. One means of achieving this is through the use of *metaphor*.

WHAT IS A METAPHOR?

One definition of a metaphor is 'understanding and experiencing one kind of thing in terms of another'.[20] What this sometimes means is describing or explaining something *abstract*, *invisible*, or *intangible* in terms of something that's *concrete*, *visible*, or *tangible*. Often, it involves 'translating' the *non-literal* into the *literal*.

It has been argued that metaphors structure how a death is seen and thought about and how we actually grieve.[21] Bereaved people aren't always able to express meanings directly: metaphors provide a means of expressing thoughts and feelings *indirectly*. The metaphors that grieving people spontaneously use often capture their actual experience better than the formal theories of grief.[22]

There are different kinds of metaphor relevant to understanding people's experience of grief. Examples of *metaphor as likening abstract feelings to concrete/physical actions* might include 'He's stuck in his grief', 'She showed signs of moving on', and 'She's left me behind'. A grieving mother, describing the abundant support and love she received from friends and colleagues following the death of her 15-year-old daughter – and only child – from MDMA (Ecstasy) wrote:

> My life goes on from here. The wheels keep turning, they need to, and although my heart is smashed into a million pieces, slowly with all this support and nurturing, I can be glued back together again.[23]

The example of 'I'm sorry for your loss' that we considered in Chapter 1 is a good illustration of *metaphor as euphemism*. Those used by bereaved people themselves might include 'I lost my husband five years ago', 'He passed away peacefully', and 'He was taken almost a year ago now'.

A common use of metaphor is to *compare grief with physical/bodily sensations*: C.S. Lewis describes the sheer physical/bodily nature of grief. The opening paragraph reads:

> No one ever told me that grief felt so much like fear. I am not afraid, but the sensation is like being afraid. The same fluttering in the stomach, the same restlessness, the yawning. I keep on swallowing.[24]

He also describes 'being mildly drunk, or concussed'.

Rachel Dixey, writing about her 33-year civil partnership with Irene (who died aged 66 from early-onset Alzheimer's disease), says 'I still feel the presence of an absence, still feel as though I've been cut in half. I wonder if twins feel like this. I know many of the widowed do'.[25] Other examples include 'being heartbroken' and 'having a broken heart'.

Other metaphors act as *similes* (i.e. 'Grief is like. . . '). Edward Hirsch, in a poem written for his dead son, describes grieving as like carrying a bag of cement up a mountain during the night.[26]

A study of hospice nurses found that they use metaphors to describe the *containment of emotion* as a way of expressing feeling both burdened and drained from repeatedly being with the dying. They spoke of being a 'sponge' and consciously distancing themselves from their emotions by stepping back, switching off, and developing a veneer.[27]

One metaphor for grief that has been proposed as a way of trying to understand it – and make it more tolerable – is a *houseguest* that arrives without invitation, infiltrating all aspects of bereaved people's lives, families, relationships, and health. The more effort made to force it out, the more intrusive it becomes:

> If, however, room is made for this houseguest, its presence becomes expected at times, its comings and goings are not surprises, its intrusions not unanticipated. In time, its presence even becomes welcome as something familiar . . . its very absence and presence serves to sustain a mutable, evolving, sometimes intermittent, but lifelong relationship with the loss.[28]

(This metaphor is consistent with the Continuing Bonds approach; see Chapter 3.)

Emily and her dying husband, Ben, referred to his cancer as a *monster* that sleeps by their bed at night; if they're lucky, it sleeps for a while in the morning before it starts demanding to be fed. They're then forced to feed it for the rest of the day. 'Monster' conveys their perception of the cancer as a terrible threat: frightening, dangerous, and insatiable, devouring life as they'd known it and literally eating up Ben's body. The metaphor helped them to *externalise* the disease; it also allowed Emily to reveal indirectly that she knew they'd eventually lose the battle. When Ben died shortly after Emily first used the metaphor, she said: 'One good thing about Ben's death is that the monster was dead too!'[29]

TONKIN'S CIRCLES

A well-known, *visual* metaphor among bereavement supporters and counsellors is what's commonly referred to as 'Tonkin's circles'.[30] A woman whose child had died some years before stated how her grief had totally consumed her. (Notice the metaphor in that last sentence.) She drew a circle to represent her life: she shaded the whole circle to indicate that her whole life had been filled with her grief. She had imagined that, as time passed, the grief would shrink and become neatly contained within her life, in a small and manageable way (represented as a second unshaded circle – her life – containing a much smaller, shaded circle – her grief). She was realistic enough to assume that the grief would never disappear altogether.

However, what happened was very different. The shaded grief circle stayed just as big, but her life grew around it (the 'life circle' was now much larger than it had been before and contained the same-sized grief circle). There were times, such as anniversaries or 'trigger' moments (i.e. reminders of her daughter), when she operated entirely from out of the grief circle; her grief felt just as intense as it ever had. But, increasingly, she was able to experience life in the larger, unshaded, circle.

One of the great strengths of this metaphor is that it relieves bereaved people of the expectation (often emanating from others) that we should 'recover' or 'get over' our grief at some point (see Chapter 1). At the same time, the enduring grief circle means that the deceased loved one remains 'with us' and we don't have to feel guilty about not being constantly overwhelmed by our grief. (Again, this metaphor is consistent with the Continuing Bonds approach.)

THE 'GRIEF-AS-A-JOURNEY' METAPHOR

Arguably, the most all-embracing metaphor for grief – and life as a whole following bereavement – is a journey. This might be the way that a bereavement supporter/counsellor construes his/her work with a bereaved client, whereby s/he accompanies the client on his/her unique journey. According to one bereavement counsellor, for older bereaved people life's journey may have lost its appeal. For younger bereaved people, the future may now seem more uncertain. For all bereaved people:

> They have perhaps lost their way, lost direction. The one who was directing them, offering stability and guidance along the way, is

no longer there. . . . They do not know how to live in this place of grief and sorrow; it is like nothing they have ever encountered before.[31]

Other related similes include *rollercoaster, river, 'long and winding' road, railway track, tidal ebb and flow, whirlpool/quicksand/earthquake/tsunami*.[32] The metaphor may be shared with the client, or the client may spontaneously produce it. In Danny Abse's diary account of his grief following his wife's (Joan's) death in a car crash, he writes, 'For intermittent hours each day I feel like an exile in the Land of Desolation'.[33] And again, while most of the time he copes and must appear 'balanced' to strangers, 'without Joan pointing direction I feel I'm lost in a foreign city and have to stop to read myself as if I were a map'.[34]

(See Chapter 5 for a description of metaphors used by couples to express their grief for the loss of their child.)

SOME OTHER ASSUMPTIONS/ MISCONCEPTIONS ABOUT GRIEF

What emerges from this evaluation of stage/phase accounts of grief is that there's no single 'grief pathway' that all bereaved people must go down. The proposed stages/phases are not prescriptive: it's not possible to say where any particular bereaved individual will be at any particular time following bereavement. Also, there's no clear end point: as the circles of grief metaphor makes clear, grief remains with us forever. Bereaved people – at least those in Western culture – don't simply 'recover' or 'get over' their loss and return to normal; there's no resolution or completion *per se*, but rather they adapt, adjust, and are to some degree changed forever.[35]

The notion of fixed stages/phases can be added to a list of four 'myths of coping with loss'[36] namely that: (i) every bereaved person necessarily shows distress and depression; (ii) the absence of these indicates pathological (or complicated) grieving (see Chapter 6); (iii) recovery always occurs given time; and (iv) 'grief work' is necessary for recovery (see Chapter 3).

Clearly, (ii), (iii), and (iv) assume that (i) is true (and can be described as the 'universalist assumption').

DOES BEREAVEMENT INEVITABLY PRODUCE DISTRESS AND DEPRESSION?

A follow-up study of a group of bereaved people, mostly widows and widowers, for up to five years, found that between 26 and 65 per cent displayed no significant symptoms of either distress (yearning for the deceased, feeling that life had lost its meaning, feeling anxious about the future, or experiencing shock at the loss) or depression (feelings of sadness, being self-critical, having suicidal thoughts, lacking energy, or disturbed sleep and eating patterns) during this period.[37]

One of the most consistent findings that has emerged from empirical tests of these 'myths' of coping with loss is that bereavement is not a one-dimensional experience; bereaved people show different patterns or trajectories of grief.[38]

THE THREE MOST COMMON PATTERNS OR TRAJECTORIES OF GRIEF

In chronic grief, the pain of loss simply overwhelms the bereaved person, who finds it almost impossible to return to his/her normal daily routine. This kind of struggle can continue for years. Recovery is a gradual process; the bereaved person suffers acutely but then slowly picks up the pieces and begins putting his/her life back together.

As frightening as the pain of loss can be, for most of us grief is not overwhelming or unending. We may be shocked, even wounded, by a bereavement, but we still manage to regain our equilibrium and move on. While we may experience anguish or sadness, there's much more involved.

> Above all, it [bereavement] is a human experience. It is something we are wired for, and it is certainly not meant to overwhelm us. Rather, our reactions to grief seem designed to help

us accept and accommodate losses relatively quickly so that we can continue to live productive lives.[39]

This is a definition of *resilience*, another of the most common trajectories.

Research involving people aged 65 and over shows that most people are resilient and don't become seriously depressed or distressed. It also confirms the common observation that in elderly people, especially among those whose partner suffered a long illness, high levels of depression often *precede* bereavement, which may sometimes come as a relief.

These findings regarding resilience have been replicated in relation to people's reactions to war, terrorist attacks, disease, natural disasters, and sexual abuse. In all these different situations, most people adapt surprisingly well to whatever the world throws at them: life returns to a measure of normality in a matter of months. Typically, in the immediate aftermath of the event, up to two thirds of those surveyed experienced few, if any, symptoms of trauma (such as sleeping difficulties, hypervigilance, or flashbacks; see Chapter 6); within six months, fewer than 10 per cent reported such symptoms. The term 'coping ugly' has been used to help explain this ability to successfully manage such (potentially) traumatic experiences.[40]

For most people, instead of getting 'stuck' in an inconsolable psychological state, the brain's alarm system (the 'fight-or-flight' syndrome) is toned down. If emotions become extreme, a kind of internal sensor (a 'resilience-stat') returns us to a more balanced state.[41]

Bereavement is a powerful experience, even for the most resilient among us: it forces us to ask questions about the world and our place in it that might never otherwise have occurred to us (see Chapter 7).

CONCLUSION: GRIEF OR GRIEVING?

As we've seen, what different people experience and how they react to a major bereavement is highly variable and individualised: this underlies one of the mantras of bereavement support/counselling, namely that everyone's *grief profile* (or 'grief journey') is unique.

When we use the word 'grief' (a noun), we're turning an experience into a 'thing' or 'entity' in order to make it easier to study in a scientific or objective way (i.e. we're reifying it). This lived experience is more validly understood as a process (denoted by the verb 'to grieve' or 'grieving'), something which changes over time, but very unpredictably.[42]

3

TRYING TO EXPLAIN GRIEF
WHAT IS IT FOR?

Stage models and theories are taken to provide a *normative* account of the grieving process, i.e. they tell how people typically grieve (*descriptive*) and how we *should* grieve (*prescriptive*). However, as noted in Chapter 2, there's no single, common, predictable course taken by every person's grief.

We also noted that there's perhaps an inevitable gap between theories of grief and people's actual experience of grief, and this is why we devoted so much space to a discussion of metaphor in Chapter 2. The use of metaphor is one way of acknowledging and exploring the individuality of people's grief.

What we focus on in this chapter is other theories and models of grief that are more concerned with the prescriptive side of the normative equation; i.e. rather than describing what grief is like, they emphasise the importance of grieving for maintaining mental – and physical – health. They focus on what grief is for, its psychological and social functions.

ATTACHMENT, LOVE, AND LOSS

Arguably, the most fundamental question we can ask about grief and grieving is: regardless of for how long, in what ways, and with what intensity, why should the death of a loved one cause us to grieve *at all*? One answer is provided like this:

> For most people, love is the most profound source of pleasure in our lives while the loss of those whom we love is the most profound sense of pain. Hence, love and loss are two sides of the same coin. We cannot have one without risking the other.[1]

However, to claim that of course we're going to grieve for those we love who die, begs a number of fundamental questions: what is love? How is a child's love for its mother related to adults' love for their sexual partners? How is a child's response to separation from its mother related to an adult's grief when a partner dies? What do those who are closest to us emotionally provide that we no longer have access to when they die?

While not actually a theory of grief, *attachment theory* has attempted to answer these questions and, for this reason, can be regarded as providing a theoretical foundation on which all later accounts of grief depend.

AN EVOLUTIONARY THEORY OF LOVE: LOVE AS ATTACHMENT

What makes attachment theory foundational in this sense is that it adopts an *ethological* or *evolutionary* perspective. Bowlby was a trained psychoanalyst (i.e. the theories and psychotherapeutic methods based on Freud) but was highly critical of Freud's explanation of attachment. For Freud, the child became attached to the mother because she feeds it – and provides its other biological (*primary*) needs; this makes attachments (or the child's love for the mother) *secondary*. (This account is known as the *cupboard love* theory.)

Bowlby was very much influenced by the work of *ethologists* (zoologists who study animal behaviour in its natural environment/habitat), in particular, Konrad Lorenz, famous for his 1930s studies of *imprinting* in goslings.[2] This inborn/innate tendency to become imprinted is equivalent to the human infant's innate tendency to become attached (i.e. emotionally tied) to the mother (or mother-figure), what Bowlby called *monotropy*.

Bowlby was also influenced by Harlow's famous experiments with rhesus monkeys conducted in the 1950s, which showed that the innate need for *contact comfort* is as basic as the need for food.[3]

An *evolutionary* account focuses on the *functions* that love evolved to meet. Compared with other primates, humans are dependent on their parents for an exceptionally long period of time. As length of child-hood (and related brain size) increased steadily over the last million years or so of human evolution, so there were strong selection pres-sures toward the development of (relatively) *monogamous pair-bonding*. In other words, 'Love is . . . an evolutionary device to persuade couples to stay together for long enough to give their children a good shot at making it to adulthood'.[4] In our hunter-gatherer ancestral environ-ment, attachment bonds between procreative partners would have greatly enhanced the survival of their offspring.

THE ATTACHMENT BEHAVIOURAL SYSTEM

Bowlby identified three basic *behavioural systems* that bond male–female pairs together: *attachment*, *caregiving*, and *sex*. So, when we say 'I love you', we can mean: (i) *love as attachment*: 'I am emotionally dependent on you for happiness, safety and security; I feel anxious and lonely when you're gone, relieved and stronger when you're near. I want to be comforted, supported emotionally, and taken care of by you'; (ii) *love as caregiving*: 'I get great pleasure from supporting, caring for and taking care of you; from facilitating your progress, health, growth and happiness'; or (iii) *love as sexual attraction*: 'I am sexually attracted to you. . . . You excite me, "turn me on", make me feel alive'.[5]

In the rest of this section – and the rest of the book – we shall be focusing on 'love as attachment'.

THE HUMAN ATTACHMENT SYSTEM

The human infant's attachment is designed to (i) provide the infant with a sense of security, enabling it to play and explore its environ-ment; and (ii) regulate how far away from the mother the child will move and how much fear it will show towards strangers.

Generally, attachment behaviours (such as cuddling, looking, smiling, crying, and trying to stay close to the mother) are more evident when the child is unwell, afraid, or in unfamiliar surroundings. When she's judged to be sufficiently available and responsive, an infant is thought to experience 'felt security'. But when she's unavailable or unresponsive, the infant becomes anxious and desperately tries to re-establish contact by calling, searching, approaching, and clinging.

THE COMPONENTS OR STAGES OF DISTRESS

Short-term separations, such as when a child goes into hospital, typically produce *distress*; this comprises three major components: *protest*, *despair*, and *detachment*.

The initial, immediate reaction involves crying, screaming, kicking, and generally struggling to escape, or clinging to the mother to prevent her from leaving. This *protest* component is an outward and direct expression of the child's anger, fear, and bewilderment. Protest is typically followed by *despair*, in which the child begins to calm down and may appear apathetic, keeping its fear and anger 'locked up' and wanting nothing to do with other people. The child barely reacts to others' offers of comfort, preferring to comfort itself by rocking, thumb-sucking, and so on.

If the separation continues, the child begins to respond to people again, but tends to treat everyone alike and rather superficially. If reunited with the mother at this stage, the child may well have to 'relearn' its relationship with her and may even 'reject' her (as she 'rejected' her child). This third stage, *detachment*, represents a *defensive* suppression of attachment behaviours – the detachment is more apparent than real.

In the hostile and unpredictable environment in which human beings (*Homo sapiens*) evolved, the protest reactions would have kept infants close to their protective caregivers; in turn, this would have increased their chances of survival. Viewed in this light, many of the apparently puzzling reactions to separation and loss (such as continuing to yearn and search even when a lost caregiver is objectively – and permanently – unavailable [i.e. dead]) seem more reasonable and, in many situations, adaptive.[6]

The same tendency to search and reunite with the attachment figure is displayed when an adult loses a loved spouse or partner; this may sometimes be expressed as the wish to die oneself in order to be reunited with the loved one and in extreme cases this natural impulse leads to suicide (see Chapter 6). Feelings of loneliness derive specifically from the absence of the attachment figure; however supportive other people may be, they cannot fill the emotional gap left by the deceased spouse/partner. Attachment bonds are *person-specific*: it's the spouse/partner him/herself who is grieved, rather than his/her role; attachments involve shared experiences and memories that are unique to a history of interactions with that particular person.

Originally, Bowlby used 'detachment' for the final phase of adult grieving. He later changed this to 'reorganisation', reflecting his belief that many bereaved people do not, and do not wish to, 'detach' defensively from their lost attachment figure. Instead, they rearrange their representations of self and the deceased loved one (their *inner working models* [IWMs]), making possible both a *continuing bond* and adjustment to life without the deceased (see the discussion of Freud's 'classical' account of grief in the next section).

INDIVIDUAL VARIATIONS IN ATTACHMENT

One of Bowlby's research students, Mary Ainsworth, was the first to investigate different *attachment styles*. Ainsworth identified three major attachment types among a sample of 1-year-olds: *anxious-avoidant* (Type A), *securely attached* (Type B), and *anxious-resistant/ambivalent* (Type C)[7] Later, a fourth attachment style was identified, namely, *insecure-disorganised* (Type D).[8] (Types A, C, and D are referred to as *insecure* attachment styles.)

Until recently, attachment (including attachment styles) was studied almost exclusively within parent-child relationships. However, Bowlby had always maintained that attachment behaviour is a feature of human beings 'from the cradle to the grave'. But clearly, attachment patterns and their consequences become much more complex by the time we reach adulthood. A groundbreaking 1987 study applied Ainsworth et al.'s three basic attachment styles to adult-adult sexual/romantic relationships, asking how an adult's attachment patterns are related to their childhood attachments to their parents.[9]

ATTACHMENT STYLES AND ADJUSTMENT TO LOSS

As noted earlier, love and loss are two sides of a coin.[10] The attachment patterns originally identified by Ainsworth et al. represent ways of *coping*: ultimately, it's the fit between a particular situation and a particular worldview that determines who will cope well and who will cope badly.

Parkes's Love and Loss Study (see Chapter 1) confirmed his impressions gained from many years as a practising psychiatrist, that people who grow up in *secure* family environments (i.e. where parents respond sensitively and promptly to their needs) experience less intense distress following bereavement than those from insecure environments. This reflects a more positive IWM, more harmonious marriages, and a greater willingness to turn to others for support.

However, the study also found that the incidence of *insecure* attachment was very similar in both the psychiatric and control samples; this suggests *either* (i) that insecure attachments played little part in causing the psychiatric problems *or* (ii) that attachment insecurity can have mixed effects. Insecure attachments can sometimes be useful ways of coping with the less-than-perfect world of adult life (including the near inevitability of suffering bereavement).

(We shall revisit attachment and loss when discussing the *dual process model* later in this chapter.)

FREUD'S GRIEF THEORY: MOURNING AS DETACHMENT

As noted in Chapter 1, Freud was one of the first to formally address the nature of grief – and its function – in *Mourning and Melancholia*. By 'melancholia' Freud meant what we would now call clinical (major) depression, a deviant, complicated, and unhealthy form of mourning (or grieving). For Freud, mourning represents the work involved in uncoupling or achieving detachment (or emancipation) from the lost person/object; this reflects both a desire to hold onto the lost object *and* a growing recognition that it is no longer available. This work is complex and can take considerable time and effort. Because the bereaved person has invested a great deal of psychic or psychological energy (*libido*) in the person or object, its loss inevitably involves pain. The goal is to withdraw libido from the lost object, thereby freeing the ego (the conscious, decision-making part of the personality) for new and healthy attachments. This is the *work of grief* – or *grief work*; its specific psychological function is to 'detach the survivor's memories and hopes from the dead'.[11]

GRIEF WORK

As with the notion of stages of grief, the notion that one 'has to do one's grief work' is well-known in popular as well as scientific literature on bereavement.[12] However, many modern researchers have questioned the 'wisdom' of this widely-held belief.

The concept of grief work refers to the cognitive processes of confronting the reality of a loss through death, of going over events that occurred before and at the time of death, and of focusing on memories and working toward detachment from (or relocating) the deceased. The bereaved person needs to bring the reality of the loss into awareness as much as possible; suppressing this reality is pathological. According to the *grief work hypothesis* (GWH), one has to confront the experience of bereavement in order to come to terms with loss and avoid detrimental health consequences.[13,14]

GRIEF WORK AND ACUTE GRIEF

Bowlby incorporated the concept of grief work into his explanation of the grieving process, as did Lindemann in his account of *acute grief*.

Typical characteristics of acute grief include somatic distress, preoccupation with the image of the deceased, guilt, hostility, and alterations in usual behaviour patterns. Many bereaved individuals also adopt traits that were possessed by the deceased, displaying them in their own behaviour. Grief work involves efforts to emancipate oneself from bondage to the deceased, readjust to an environment in which the deceased is missing, and form new relationships.

Trying to avoid the intense distress involved in the experience of grief may only inhibit and complicate grief work. In turn, delaying or distorting grief reactions lead to morbid or unhealthy forms of grief.

Working through grief is important for the purpose of adapting one's IWMs of the lost person and the self. Although this enables 'detachment' or 'reorganisation' (see page 31), or the breaking of affectional bonds,[15] at the same time it also strengthens the *continuation* of the bond (a relocation of the deceased so that adjustment to his/her physical absence can gradually be made).

AN EVALUATION OF THE GWH

It's not surprising that the notion of grief work has been so influential both theoretically and in the applied field, even to the extent that it has become a 'blueprint' for coping with grief.[16] As we saw when quoting Shakespeare in Chapter 2, it seems intuitively true that we must 'give sorrow words'; expressing grief (in any form, but especially in words) is essential.

However, there are four major shortcomings associated with the GWH.[17] 'Grief work' isn't clearly defined (e.g. the confounding of negatively-associated *rumination* and more positively-associated aspects of 'working through'); this makes it difficult to *measure* particular aspects of GW (such as yearning and pining). There's also a lack of sound evidence in support of grief work: not only is there little evidence that confronting grief predicts adaptation, but evidence exists showing that working through could actually be detrimental to adaptation.[18] Finally, it's doubtful whether GW is a *universal* feature of human grief (see Chapter 4).

Also, while grief work was a fundamental notion underlying the development of stage/phase models (see Chapter 2), the process itself, as these models describe it, seems rather *passive*: the person appears to be 'put through' the stages, neglecting the active, effortful struggle which is so much part of grieving. They also don't allow for any respite: grief is arduous and exhausting, and a 'break' can be recuperative.[19] By focusing exclusively on the *primary loss*, namely, the deceased person, the GWH neglects the many *secondary losses* which, collectively (if not individually), can demand as much, if not greater, adjustment (see Chapter 1).

THE TASKS OF MOURNING

Mourning should be thought of as an active *process* (rather than a state), comprising four tasks.[20] Although the tasks don't necessarily follow a specific order, the names of the tasks imply a sequence. For example, you cannot handle the emotional impact of a loss until you have first come to terms with the fact that the loss has happened.

According to Worden, the first task is to *acknowledge and accept the reality of the death*. The searching behaviour as described extensively by Bowlby and Parkes (see page 31 and Chapter 2) is directly related to this task. Denial can take various forms, but it most often involves the details, meaning, or irreversibility of the loss. One example of denial is *mummification*,[21] in which the bereaved person keeps the deceased's possessions in a mummified condition ready for use when s/he returns (such as keeping the loved one's room exactly as it was before the death).

The second task is to *experience/process the pain of grief*. It's appropriate to experience pain during bereavement, provided this doesn't become overwhelming. The pain is both literal (i.e. physical) and emotional, as well as spiritual (see Chapter 2). It's necessary to acknowledge and work through this pain or it will manifest itself through some symptom or other form of aberrant behaviour. It's impossible to lose someone we've been deeply attached to without experiencing *some* degree of pain.

The third task involves *adjusting to a world without the deceased*. Bereaved individuals engage in a voyage of discovery to determine the significance of the now-severed relationship, to identify each of the various roles the deceased played in the relationship, to adjust to the fact that the deceased is no longer available to fill those roles, and often to develop new skills to fulfil the deceased's former roles. The bereaved person is usually not aware of all the roles played by the deceased until after his/her death.

The fourth and final task is to *find an enduring connection with the deceased in the midst of embarking on a new life*. The main point is to encourage bereaved people to modify or restructure their relationship with the deceased in ways that remain satisfying but that also reflect the changed circumstances of life following a bereavement. This task requires bereaved individuals to rethink their personal identity, restructure their relationship with the deceased in the light of the loss, avoid becoming neurotically burdened by the past in ways that diminish future quality of life, and remain open to new attachments and other relationships.

Many people – especially bereaved spouses – find this the most difficult of the four tasks. They think that if they withdraw their emotional attachment, they are somehow dishonouring the memory of the deceased. They may get stuck at this point in their grieving.

These tasks reflect an interpretation of mourning as, in principle, a *proactive* way of striving to manage one's loss and grief, a means of enabling the bereaved person to regain some degree of control.[22] Note also that grief work *doesn't* require a total severing of the attachment to the deceased loved one: the relationship continues but in a redefined way.

PSYCHOSOCIAL TRANSITION THEORY (PSTT): GRIEF AS ADAPTING TO CHANGE

> Grief is essentially an emotion that draws us toward something or someone that is missing. It arises from awareness of a discrepancy between the world that is and the world that 'should be'.[23]

The world that should be is an internal construct, which means that each person's experience of grief is individual and unique.

PSYCHOSOCIAL TRANSITIONS

The most dangerous life-change events as far as mental health is concerned (or *psychosocial transitions* [PSTs]) are those that have long-lasting implications, take place over a relatively short time-scale (allowing little chance to prepare), and that require people to undertake a major revision of their *assumptive world* (everything we take for granted about the world – including ourselves and other people – based on our past experience).

> The death of a spouse invalidates assumptions that penetrate many aspects of life, from the moment of rising to going to sleep in an empty bed. Habits of action . . . and thought . . . must be revised if the survivor is to live as a widow.[24]

Like all habits, these habits of action and thought have become *automatic*; this makes change very difficult. Grief following bereavement is aggravated if the deceased is the person one would normally turn to in times of trouble: faced with the worst imaginable situation, we may repeatedly find ourselves turning toward a person who isn't there. The familiar world suddenly seems to have become unfamiliar and we lose confidence in our own internal world.

> A person is literally lost in his or her own grief, and the more disorganised one's thinking the more difficult it is to step aside from the disorganisation and to see clearly what is lost and what remains.[25]

People who have lost confidence in their model of the world feel very unsafe; anxiety and fear cloud their judgement and impair concentration and memory.

Almost by definition, PSTs involve a large number of simultaneous dysfunctions in several areas of functioning (i.e. *secondary losses*). Thus, the death of a spouse may produce any or all of the following losses: sexual partner, protection from danger, reassurance of worth, companionship, income, recreational partner, status, expectations, self-confidence, home, and parent for one's children. However, it may also produce relief from responsibilities, entitlement to care and sympathy of others, and freedom to realise potentialities that have been inhibited.

PSTT AND TRAUMA

Most studies of the psychological consequences of bereavement have shown that deaths that are (i) sudden; (ii) unexpected; and (iii) untimely are more likely to create problems than those that have been anticipated and prepared for. Other factors that contribute to complicated grief include witnessing violence or mutilation, deaths for which someone is to blame (including murders and suicides), and those in which no intact body is recovered. These are all examples of *traumatic losses* (see Chapter 6).

The Harvard Study (see Chapter 1) found that unexpected and untimely bereavements in young widows and widowers were associated, in the short term, with greater disbelief and avoidance of confrontation with the loss. Over time, there was a persisting sense of the presence of the deceased spouse, a feeling of continued obligation to them and social withdrawal along with constant anxiety, depression, loneliness, and, often, self-reproach. All of these were less common in those who'd anticipated their loss.

PSTT AND ATTACHMENT THEORY

If attachment theory explains the urge to cry and to search for someone who is lost, and PSTT explains the need to rethink and replan one's life in the face of a major change, how are these two alternatives worked out in the moment-to-moment life of bereaved people?

The answer is to be found in the *dual process model* to which we now turn.[26]

DUAL PROCESS MODEL: OSCILLATION BETWEEN LOSS AND RESTORATION

The dual process model (DPM) of coping with bereavement emerged from the growing concern among bereavement theorists, during the

1990s in particular, about the adequacy of the GWH as an explanation of effective coping. In addition to the criticisms considered above (see pages 34–35), two further concerns are (i) whether the observed phenomena of grieving are adequately represented in the GWH; and (ii) its lack of general application.[27]

Regarding the inadequate representation of bereavement-related phenomena, the GWH focuses on the need to confront the primary loss, while paying little attention to both the tendency to avoid this and all the associated secondary losses (or stressors). Also, while the GWH presents grief work as a purely internal, intrapersonal process, the dynamic process of coming to terms with a death does not take place in isolation. The bereaved person is surrounded by others, some of whom are themselves grieving; hence, grieving takes place at both the intrapersonal and interpersonal levels.

A grief work framework implicitly assumes that, following the death of a loved one, one must return to a positive state of mind and well-being as quickly as possible. In turn, this implies that human suffering is bad and that the human condition should only, ideally, involve positive states and emotions. This view is far from universal (see Chapter 4).

In relation to gender, the GWH doesn't take sufficient account of preferred masculine ways of going about grieving, which are typically less overtly expressive of distress and depression compared with female responses. In Chapter 1, we referred to typical male and female styles of grieving as instrumental and intuitive, respectively; as noted, while gender influences grieving style, it doesn't determine it (otherwise there'd be no exceptions to the gender 'rule').

Also, the GWH was based on the study of largely female samples; this implies that the GWH is a 'female model of grieving' and so begs the question as to whether or not it applies to male grievers.

Similarly, the GWH is culture-bound, at least with respect to the overt level of grief. Different views regarding acceptable or 'healthy' ways of coping can be found in non-Western cultures. Some cultures show little or no evidence of 'working through' patterns: this apparently would be considered detrimental to the health of the bereaved and those around them (cultural differences are discussed in greater detail in Chapter 4).

THE MAIN COMPONENTS OF THE DPM

Unlike earlier models, the DPM was originally formulated to address, specifically, coping with loss of a spouse; more recently, it has come to be applied to *all* types of bereavement, including loss of a child, and to bereavement specifically among the elderly. It might also be relevant to understanding *homesickness*, which can be thought of as a 'mini-grief' experience.[28]

As well as providing a model of *coping* with loss, the DPM was also aimed at better understanding individual differences in how people come to terms with this most stressful of life events. The DPM makes a fundamental distinction between two categories of bereavement-related stressors, namely, *loss-oriented* versus *restoration-oriented* stressors.

Loss-orientation refers to the bereaved person's concentration on, appraisal of, and processing of some aspect of the loss experience itself (i.e. the *primary* stressor) and, as such, incorporates grief work. It involves a painful yearning for, even searching for, the lost person, a phenomenon that lies at the heart of grieving. Other features include rumination about the life shared with the deceased, and the circumstances and events surrounding the death. A range of emotional reactions are involved, from pleasurable reminiscing to painful longing, from happiness that the deceased is no longer suffering to despair that one is left alone.

Restoration-orientation refers to the focus on *secondary* stressors that are also consequences of the bereavement, reflecting a struggle to reorient oneself in a changed world without the deceased person. Rethinking and replanning one's life in the face of bereavement can also be regarded as an essential feature of grieving (see the discussion of PSTT). The focus is on *what* needs to be dealt with (e.g. social isolation) and *how* it is dealt with (e.g. by joining social organisations), rather than the *result* of this process (e.g. restored well-being and social integration). As with the loss orientation, a wide range of emotions can be involved, from relief and pride at mastering a new skill or taking the courage to go out alone, to fear and anxiety that one will not succeed, or despair at the loneliness of being with others and yet being 'single'.

OSCILLATION

Both orientations are sources of stress and can be associated with outcomes such as distress and anxiety; both are also involved in the coping process. The process of attending to or avoiding these two types of stressor is dynamic and fluctuating. This dynamic coping process is called *oscillation*.

The principle underlying oscillation is that at times, the bereaved person will confront aspects of loss, and at other times avoid them; the same applies to restoration tasks. Also, there will sometimes be 'time out', when the person is not grieving at all. Therefore, coping with bereavement is a complex regulatory process of confrontation and avoidance, and oscillation between the two types of stressors is necessary for adaptive coping.

Clearly, the DPM is not a stage or phase account of grief; rather, it sees grief as waxing and waning over time. Early on in bereavement, the loss orientation dominates; later, attention turns increasingly to secondary losses and restoration. For example, early on there's generally relatively little attention given to forming a new identity and far more to going over the circumstances of the death; over time, a gradual reversal in attention to these different concerns is likely to occur. Also, over time, the total amount of time spent on coping with loss and restoration tasks will decrease.

EVALUATION OF THE DPM

'Restoration' is *not* about trying to recreate the bereaved person's former world of lived experiences (which no longer exists) or the old assumptive world (which has also been shattered by the loss). Rather, it has to do with efforts to adapt to the new world in which bereaved individuals find themselves. What is restored, therefore, is not a past mode of living, but the ability to live productively in the present and future.[29]

DPM AND COMPLICATED GRIEF

The model provides a framework for understanding complicated or pathological forms of grief (such as *chronic, absent,* or *inhibited*). In earlier models, these forms of grief weren't nearly so differentiated or explicit, with chronic grievers focusing on loss-oriented, absent grievers on restoration-oriented, activities; those who suffer a complicated form of traumatic bereavement might be expected to have trouble alternating smoothly between the two orientations, and manifesting extreme symptoms of intrusion and avoidance. However, in both loss-oriented (e.g. chronic) and restoration-oriented (e.g. absent) types of complicated grief, *reactions are extreme,* focusing excessively on one orientation and avoiding the other. These patterns are *very different* from the confrontation-avoidance oscillation that the DPM sees as characteristic of 'normal' coping with bereavement. Such pathological forms of grieving can be regarded as disturbances of oscillation (see Chapter 6).

DPM, COMPLICATED GRIEF, AND ATTACHMENT THEORY

The relationship between complicated grief and patterns of attachment have recently been discussed within the context of DPM. For example, the DPM predicts that the extent to which bereaved individuals will engage in either loss-oriented or restoration-oriented processes depends on various factors, in particular their attachment styles (see pages 31–32).

Securely attached individuals are expected to be able to access their attachment-related emotional memories without difficulty and to be able to discuss them coherently, thus presenting normal grief reactions. They would be expected to display healthy oscillation between loss- and restoration-related activities.

Anxious-avoidant individuals would suppress and avoid attachment-related emotions and present absent or inhibited grief reactions, behaving as if nothing had happened and focusing on restoration-related activities. The bond with the deceased would be too *loose*.[30] (It's also been pointed out by several writers that absent grief doesn't always or necessarily indicate pathological processes: it might actually indicate that the attachment with the deceased wasn't sufficiently strong to produce grief, or that s/he is no longer grieving.)

Anxious-ambivalent individuals are expected to be highly emotional, clinging to ties with the deceased; they would focus on the loss-orientation to the exclusion of restoration-related activities (i.e. chronic grief). The bond with the deceased would be too *strong*.

Disorganised individuals would be unable to think and talk coherently about attachment-related memories and would show *traumatic grief* reactions.[31]

Anxiously-attached individuals can be thought of as *hyperaroused* (i.e. experiencing emotional 'overwhelm', panic, impulsivity, and anger) and avoidantly-attached individuals as *hypoaroused* (i.e. numb, disconnected, and shut down).[32] This would subsequently impact on bereavement outcomes, specifically, the ability to meet the challenges in an integrated way (i.e. oscillating between loss and restoration orientations).

DPM AND GENDER DIFFERENCES

The DPM accommodates male and female differences in ways of grieving better than earlier models. Women appear to be more loss-oriented, feeling and expressing their distress (i.e. they focus more on the *primary* loss), while men are more restoration-oriented, actively engaging with the *secondary* losses. These tendencies may generally work well, unless there's a lack of oscillation.

Women's tendency toward intuitive grief fits very neatly with the DPM's description of them as more loss-oriented. Similarly, men are more likely to be instrumental grievers, consistent with their tendency to be more restoration-oriented. For example, in a heterosexual couple who lose a child, the more loss-oriented mother may perceive the more restoration-oriented father to be 'grieving less than I am', rather than simply grieving *differently*. The mother's attribution could impact negatively on the couple's adjustment to the child's death.[33] Men whose wives were, like themselves, high in restoration-oriented coping, have been found to display positive adjustment.[34] This demonstrates the role of *interpersonal factors* in coping and adjustment.

DPM AND CULTURAL DIFFERENCES

Cultural differences in the norms governing the manifestations and expressions of grief can be understood in terms of loss- versus restoration-oriented coping. For example, the Muslim community on the island of Bali would be described as restoration-oriented, showing little or no overt signs of grief and continuing daily life as though nothing untoward had happened. By contrast, Muslim people in Egypt express their grief openly, gathering together to reminisce and share anguish over their loss[35] (see Chapter 4 for other examples).

CONTINUING BONDS: ATTACHMENT AFTER DEATH

As noted, Bowlby used the term 'reorganisation' to replace the earlier 'detachment' to refer to the final stage of adult grief. For Bowlby, a continuing bond *and* adjustment to life without him/her are both possible. While Freud argued that the deceased loved one must be *completely* 'given up' (*decathexis*), Bowlby's 'detachment' allows for some continuation of the attachment with him/her.

Klass et al.'s *Continuing Bonds: New Understandings of Grief* is, arguably, the most frequently cited source of rejection of the 'detachment hypothesis'. However, the editors and most of the authors mistakenly bracket Freud and Bowlby together as advocating the detachment hypothesis, thereby defining themselves in contrast or opposition to attachment theory.[36]

The grief reactions that many psychoanalytically-oriented therapists apparently viewed as immature or pathological – searching, yearning, and sometimes expressing anger or ambivalence toward the lost attachment figure – are aspects of the normal functioning of the attachment system.[37] Bereaved individuals are commonly 'caught out' by memories of the lost loved one that seem to take them by surprise (what C.S. Lewis described as 'a sudden jab of red-hot memory'[38]). This kind of 'jab' is a normal part of coming to terms with a loss that isn't yet fully represented in all of a bereaved person's unconscious and preconscious memories; in turn, these memories are part of the IWMs of the lost attachment figure. The emotional charge associated with these unexpected memories typically decreases over time (they become less 'red-hot') – partly due to habituation and desensitisation, partly to becoming more realistic and updated. But the bereaved person's attachment to the deceased is hardly erased from memory.

The process of working through grief can be interpreted as one of emotional *neutralisation* – not forgetting.[39]

> Failure to recognise that a continuing sense of the dead person's presence . . . is a common feature of healthy mourning has led to much confused theorising . . . findings in regard both to the high prevalence of a continuing sense of the presence of the dead person and to its compatibility with a favourable outcome give no support to Freud's . . . 'its [mourning's] function is to detach the survivor's memories and hopes from the dead' (SE 13, p. 65).[40]

Bowlby was talking about Continuing Bonds (CBs) 16 years before the publication of *Continuing Bonds*.[41]

SUBSEQUENT THEORY AND RESEARCH INTO CBs

Research suggests that CBs can be either secure or insecure (in particular, part of unresolved/disorganised attachment), and there's a huge difference between (i) thinking positively about a deceased attachment figure's admirable and loving qualities and incorporating some of these into oneself, and (ii) being haunted by the deceased's sudden (imagined) appearance or being confused about whether s/he is or isn't still available in the physical world.

Most empirical studies focus on concrete aspects of CBs (such as keeping the deceased's clothes or possessions or keeping him/her in mind in various ways); as such, they don't help to distinguish healthy from unresolved grief. The effects of CBs on adjustment may depend on the length of time since bereavement. Evidence suggests that having an emotional tie with the deceased can be comforting once the acute period of grief has passed.

The idea that death does not sever the relationship to the deceased but transforms it took hold after the publication of Continuing Bonds. (It seems 'obvious' to me that we continue to have a relationship with the person who has died. Although we usually think of 'relationships' as two-way processes, aren't we engaging in a relationship when we wonder how s/he would have responded to a particular situation or ask what his/her attitude would have been to something we've done or a decision we've made? I can still hear the voices of my parents and friends who have died, enabling me to have 'conversations' with them!)

The general acceptance of the CB paradigm is a welcome development in the theoretical and clinical understanding of bereavement. Just as importantly, much CB-related research has focused on the parent-child bond: the ongoing relationships of children to their deceased parents – and siblings – has provided a dramatic alternative to the more typically studied loss of a spouse (see Chapter 5).

4

GRIEF AS A SOCIO-CULTURAL PHENOMENON
HOW SHOULD WE GRIEVE?

So far, we've discussed grief as essentially a *subjective* (private) experience (which is expressed overtly to varying degrees); this reflects the dominance of psychology in the twentieth century. By contrast with sociology, which focuses on social institutions and society as a whole, most of psychology (even social psychology) takes the *individual* as its focal point.

Turning psychology on its head, anthropology *starts* with the outward, socially sanctioned, expression of grief (mourning; see Chapter 1). In this chapter, we move from what goes on inside the head of the bereaved individual (including differences between individuals) to widely-shared attitudes and practices surrounding death within whole societies or, more commonly, sub-groups within those societies.

In between the individual mourner and the sub-group(s) is the *family unit*. It has become something of a truism among those who study bereavement, and those professionals who support people through their grief, that it is the family that's bereaved, rather than the individual. So, in order to understand and support an individual family member, it's necessary to know how the family *as a system* (or unit) has been affected by the bereavement.

At an even more general level, there's a crucial connection between grief and *culture*, the human-made part of the environment which includes language, belief systems (including religion), social practices and patterns, and social norms. Cultures differ in their very idea of reality, including the meaning, definition, and explanation of death; related to these realities are norms regarding appropriate ways of grieving.

All cultures and sub-cultures have to deal with death, psychologically, practically, and socially, and this chapter will emphasise the most widely practised rituals of mourning. But to understand those rituals, we need first to understand the widely-held attitudes towards death itself which form a major part of the social context of grief.

WESTERN SOCIETY'S ATTITUDE TOWARDS DEATH

During the nineteenth century, grief was regarded as a condition of the human soul or spirit rather than of the body; in this sense, it could neither be *normalised* nor *medicalised*.[1] But all that was to change, beginning with Freud, who was the first to distinguish between normal and pathological responses to bereavement (see Chapters 3 and 6).

THE MEDICALISATION OF GRIEF

Lindemann was the first to establish a 'symptomatology' of acute grief, which he regarded as a distinct syndrome with both psychological and somatic (bodily) symptoms (see Chapter 3). He distinguished between those people suffering from normal and morbid (pathological) grief in terms of intensity and duration; grief *management* was discussed exclusively in terms of the principles of clinical medicine.[2]

An even more extreme attempt to reduce grief to a bodily disease directly compared it to pathogenic bacteria.[3]

THE NORMALISATION OF GRIEF

Stage/phase accounts of grief have been described as adopting the *developmental metaphor*: grief is (implicitly) likened to stages of development that children naturally go through.[4,5] While only meant as averages or approximations, each stage is reached at a particular age. So, by analogy with these developmental stages, grief is seen as *unfolding* (naturally) within the human (mainly adult) psyche.

GRIEF AND SOCIAL STRUCTURE

Rejecting this 'unfolding' view, Emile Durkheim, the influential nineteenth century French sociologist, social psychologist, and philosopher, argued that grief is caused by *social processes*; these tend to channel grief into some directions while deflecting it away from others.[6]

Consistent with Durkheim's view, some researchers have acknowledged that sociological factors impinge on the intensity and duration of grief. For example, the loss of babies and (widowed) old people is less disruptive than the loss of those in economically active groups and/or the married.[7] Similarly, Durkheim argued that the intensity of grief (individual or group) depended on a socially constructed formula. This claim is consistent with anthropological studies of rituals surrounding funerals and burial rites. One example is a study of the Andaman Islanders (in the Bay of Bengal), for whom social bonds were asserted and emphasised in public declarations: without the bond, there could be no weeping. So, children who hadn't yet been awarded a social personality, were 'little mourned', and 'a stranger who dies or is killed is buried unceremoniously or is cast into the sea'.[8]

These and other anthropological and historical examples demonstrate that:

> Grief, at least in its public manifestations, is socially variable and . . . the social location of a deceased person has much to do with the manner in which grief is expressed. . . . All public expressions of grief act as a mirror in which private feelings are reflected.[9]

IS DEATH THE FINAL TABOO?

According to the British anthropologist Geoffrey Gorer, modern mourning practices are marked by a total lack of ritual. In the England of the 1960s, 'the most typical reaction [to death] is ... the denial of mourning'. If problematic experiences such as bereavement are not handled ritually, individuals will incur psychological problems, and death will resurface socially in the form of an obsession with horror comics, war movies, and disasters ('the pornography of death').[10]

Gorer, and the French amateur historian, Philippe Aries, are by far the most often quoted academic advocates of the view that death is taboo and uniquely badly handled by modern society.[11] Gorer's argument helps explain how the media can be obsessed with death even at a time when individuals find it impossible to talk about their own personal grief, and how death can be taboo, but his bereaved interviewees were so eager to talk (he'd given them 'permission' and an opportunity). His taboo thesis could even explain the continuing flood of academic material on death that has developed, especially in the U.S., since the 1950s.

However, Gorer has been widely criticised, partly for romanticising Victorian mourning rituals, and it has been suggested that the modern denial of death began in the early nineteenth, not the twentieth, century.[12]

Like Gorer, Aries argues that death is inevitably problematic. Along with sex, it's one of the major ways in which 'nature' threatens 'culture', making it necessary to 'tame' it; society traditionally achieves this through religion and ritual. But over the past few centuries, individualism, romanticism, and secularism have undermined the rituals, and the modern individual is left naked before death's obscenity. Today, we are the heirs to both a Victorian romanticism which made the loss of the loved one unbearable, and of a twentieth century denial that forbids, or at least conceals, death. This 'inheritance' can explain the apparent opposing trends in the U.S.: (i) hospitals' implicit denial of death and lack of mourning; and (ii) the continuing tradition of viewing the body.[13]

Several alternative modifications or critiques of the taboo thesis have been proposed, aimed at helping us to understand the complexity of changing attitudes and practices toward death.[14] One of these ('not forbidden, but hidden') focuses on demographic structure.

In the modern world, most deaths are of elderly people; in past generations, the vast majority of adults who died did so in the prime of life. The result is that we miss the deceased *less* than in previous centuries, making elaborate rites of passage, or even beliefs in an afterlife, less necessary. However, if fulfilled death in old age is now the norm, the more unprepared we are for atypical deaths (of children and adolescents, non-elderly spouses, traumatic deaths, etc.). Bereavement support is offered to increasingly *isolated* mourners who have suffered these *categories* of loss (see Chapters 5 and 6).

According to the *universal taboo*, the denial of death is not a modern condition, but part of the *human* condition. Both social life, and the life of individuals, would be impossible if we didn't repress our death terror.[15]

A third alternative focuses on the relationship between the *individual and society*. In traditional societies, where identity is rooted in the group more than in the individual, death doesn't threaten the individual to the extent that it does in advanced societies; in the former, death threatens groups and their culture – hence the need for communal death rituals. The reverse applies in modern societies, where identity is invested largely within the individual who is indeed threatened by death. Communal and religious death rituals that once functioned to affirm culture fall into disuse; individual therapy and one-to-one bereavement counselling aim to support bewildered individuals. Modern cultures deal with death well – it's *individual* members who struggle with it.

THE PROFESSIONALISATION OF DEATH

In comparing the way that death was dealt with in Staithes, a small coastal town in North Yorkshire in 1900, with modern practices in that same town, perhaps the most significant innovation is the emergence of a number of specialist organisations which are concerned with the processes of death and dying. This is a transformation that has stripped the family of one of its traditional functions: some of the familial and communal rituals previously associated with the death of a villager have disappeared beneath a general trend of *professionalisation*.[16]

For most residents, contact with death takes place at a distance or through intermediaries, in the form of bureaucratically-organised agencies; these perform the tasks and duties previously performed by the family or community. The very existence of these agencies implies that competence to deal with the practical matters associated with death requires professional training; this means that any relevant skills that families might have are inferior. Professionalisation has thereby resulted in a vastly different set of responses to the problem of death. The 'undertaker' has now become a 'funeral director', implying a much more professional set of skills and responsibilities.

While most people used to die at home, we are now most likely to die either in hospital, a geriatric unit, or a residential home. When death occurs in one of these institutions, the body is commonly removed to the funeral director's memorial house, rather than to the deceased's home; preparation of the body and laying-out is also performed by the funeral director rather than by the traditional female specialists in the village. Similarly, making the coffin, once a task for the local joiner, is now arranged by the funeral director, as may be the ordering of flowers and wreaths.

This professionalisation of death – and the facts regarding where most people die – can be seen as one way in which death is *hidden*. It goes hand-in-hand with what is sometimes called the *sanitisation* of death: the 'messy reality' of death which used to be dealt with by the family and the community as a whole is now removed from those social groups to the professionals, in particular hospital staff and funeral directors. Depending on the details and circumstances of the death, it's probably the norm for even the closest relatives to not actually see the deceased's body; we take it on trust that the body in the coffin is that of our loved one because we have given up what were previously the responsibilities and duties of the family to the 'death professionals'.

DEATH AND THE FAMILY

Having discussed how families are no longer involved in the practical aspects of death (at least in Western countries), we now turn to the social psychological impact of death on the family.

Death is a family event. It occurs within the context of existing relationships and family dynamics. While grief is often viewed as a personal experience, it occurs in two realms simultaneously – the intrapsychic level and the interpersonal level.[17]

Personal grief always occurs within a social context and is embedded in a web of complex relationships; in most societies, the closest relationships and attachments are found within family systems, be it the nuclear family (parents and biological offspring) typical of Western cultures or the extended family, more typical of non-Western cultures. However, this distinction between nuclear and extended families represents a gross oversimplification.

THE COMPLEX VARIETY OF WESTERN FAMILIES

While a husband and wife and their (2.5) biological children used to be the norm in Western countries, changes in both technology and social attitudes and behaviours mean that such family groupings are probably in the minority.

If single-parent families represent one end of a continuum, blended families could be seen as representing the other end: two parents who have previously been divorced or had children with a previous partner raise one or more of their children from those previous relationships together within a single family grouping. There may be full-, half-, and step-siblings all living under one roof.

While adoption has been taking place for many generations, assisted reproduction families are a relatively recent phenomenon. This can take a variety of forms, including in-vitro fertilisation (IVF), surrogacy, and donor insemination. Since the 1970s, many of the beneficiaries of donor insemination and surrogacy have been lesbian couples and – more recently – the increasing number of gay couples (who are also increasingly adopting).

FAMILY SYSTEMS THEORY

According to family systems theory (FST), families are whole entities, both unique and greater than the sum of their individual family members. Individual behaviour cannot be understood in isolation but only within the context of the social group(s) to which the individual belongs: while the experience of grief is a personal event for individuals, it is also a *systems* event for the family.

In order to understand how bereavement affects the family system, we must consider individual family members, their relationships to each other, their individual relationships with the deceased, and their relationships and interactions with other individuals and systems outside the family. Family systems comprise *sub-systems*, such as marital, sibling, and parent-child relationships. The death of a family member can have a powerful impact not only on the family system as a whole but also on the sub-system(s) which the deceased belonged to.

A death changes the family system's equilibrium, often disrupting its functioning and affecting available emotional and physical resources. For example, the death of a spouse may alter the extended kinship network (such as the surviving spouse's relationships with his/her children), the death of a child may alter perceptions of the future (including the parents' relationship with each other), and the death of a parent or breadwinner can threaten a family's sense of security (see Chapter 5).

THE IMPORTANCE OF TIMING

The timing of a bereavement in the family lifecycle can be a critical factor in how the family adjusts to the loss. Deaths that are untimely, such as those involving children, adolescents, or non-elderly adults (whether sudden or not, and whether traumatic or due to natural causes) are especially difficult.

Loss can also coincide with other major life events that pose unique challenges. For example, loss of a spouse can occur near the time of birth of a first child (such as when a police officer is killed on duty), or when the family is facing financial difficulties due to redundancy/unemployment. Multiple stressors, developmental demands, and related losses can produce overload and compromise the family's ability to cope with the bereavement.

HEALTHY FAMILY PROCESSES FOLLOWING BEREAVEMENT

Key family responses to bereavement include sharing the loss, maintaining open communication, reorganising and regaining equilibrium, and making effective use of available support systems and external resources.

Funerals, memorial services, and other post-death ceremonies can serve as meaningful occasions for family members to come together to acknowledge and share the loss of a loved one (see the next section). Both before and after a death, family members need to share deep feelings and create stronger bonds, but they must be accepting and supportive of the range of feelings that may be expressed. This can be seen as a symbolic process of creating and sharing *meaning*, in which family members have an impact on each other (it's *transactional*). Certain types of loss, such as suicide, may evoke anger and shame that may be particularly difficult to share with others; this lack of open communication may increase the possibility of blame, guilt, and conflict (see Chapter 6).

As noted in Chapter 1, death — especially if it's sudden and unexpected — inevitably produces a number of *secondary losses* (such as moving house, changing jobs, or seeking employment). These examples illustrate an age-appropriate redistribution of roles and responsibilities.

Finally, the immediate family can be helped by accessing and accepting the support of extended family and friends, religious institutions, community and mental health services, and formal support organisations such as Compassionate Friends (in both the U.K. and U.S.) and Cruse Bereavement Care (in the U.K.). Churches, mosques, synagogues, and other religious centres provide time-honoured rituals surrounding death that can provide comfort for families and connect them with others who share their belief system.

POSITIVE AND NEGATIVE OUTCOMES

The manifestations and duration of any one member's grief may be quite different from those of another (the *dissynchrony of grief*).[18]

A 'classic' demonstration of this dissynchrony is the case of parents who have lost a child: they may be so absorbed in their individual grief that they fail to reach out to each other or to provide emotional support for their remaining children. In such cases, a surviving child may assume a parental role, trying to care for all other family members, thus compromising his/her own development[19] (see Chapter 6).

Despite the inevitable pain associated with loss, there's also evidence of positive outcomes. For example, bereaved parents might express feeling more sensitive and more spiritual as a result of their loss, perceiving themselves as stronger and more mature, and placing a higher priority on family and less on money and work. These outcomes all represent the *meaning* that can be found in people's suffering. Surviving a common loss as a family can produce a renewed sense of closeness and unity, and a better understanding of each other's strengths (see Chapter 7).

FUNERALS AND OTHER DEATH-RELATED CEREMONIES

Every known culture has rituals to mark death, to acknowledge the life of the deceased, provide support for survivors, and facilitate ongoing life after such loss. Whether formal or informal, such rituals can be of therapeutic value, helping to facilitate emotional healing and family cohesion. Funeral rituals can help in accepting the reality of the loss, serve as an affirmation of faith, religious beliefs, and/or philosophy of life, facilitate emotional expression, and provide a context for emotional support from family, friends, and the wider community.[20]

A ritual can be defined as a specific behaviour or activity that gives *symbolic expression* to feelings and thoughts. Actions that occur many months or even years following a death can be thought of as rituals, such as going through the deceased's personal belongings or taking off a wedding ring; these have important symbolic significance, even if performed privately with no one else to witness them. Rituals can also provide a context for *reminiscence*, which can be performed privately, but when shared with another person can represent an important aspect of social support.[21]

FUNERALS AND GRIEF WORK

Compared with the U.K., it's quite common for relatives in the U.S. to view the body before the funeral in a chapel of rest in order to 'pay their respects' and say 'goodbye'. The financial costs associated with this practice have led some U.S. critics to accuse funeral directors of exploitation, quite apart from the pointlessness of trying to make a corpse look 'life-like' or producing an illusion of sleep.[22]

However, physical death and social death don't take place simultaneously: 'grief is a process of realisation, of "making real" the fact of loss. This process takes time'.[23] Anything that *forces* reality-testing in the early post-bereavement period is likely to cause problems, especially in the case of sudden and traumatic death; these problems may include panic attacks, the massive shutting off of emotion, and/or the repetitious reliving of the traumatic events as in post-traumatic stress disorder (PTSD). However, the disturbing memories of a painful death or a mutilated body can be mitigated to some degree by positive memories of the funeral.[24]

For many of the young widows in the London Study (see Chapter 1), the funeral service (within a week of bereavement) took place too soon after the death to be of great positive psychological value (a successful *rite de passage*). However, it brought family and friends together to be close to the widow, and over half of the participants referred to the support this provided as a positive experience.

> One of the most important purposes [of the funeral] is to facilitate grief work. Grief begins with acceptance, with facing up. People need to come to grips with the reality of the death. This acceptance must not only be intellectual, it must also be emotional.[25]

BURIAL OR CREMATION?

Although funerals may be more for the living than the deceased, whether cremation or burial takes place may reflect the expressed wishes of the deceased. In the London Study, although some widows subsequently visited the crematorium, entered their husband's name in the Book of Remembrance, and attended memorial services, there was a tendency to feel less close to him at the crematorium than at the cemetery. Several widows regarded this as a distinct disadvantage of cremation. (Of course, in some parts of the world, notably the Indian sub-continent, cremation is the norm.)

WHERE DO THE DEAD 'GO'?

Traditionally, in all major religions, what matters most is the *destination of the soul*.[26] Most funerals and similar rituals end by indicating a location for the dead, a grave, shrine, or similar place where bereaved people can 'visit' them, communicate with them, and, to some degree, continue to care for them. While such places are a poor substitute for the physical presence of the dead loved one, they often give comfort and are seen as mitigating some of the pain of separation.

This sense of the dead having a physical, tangible location may help to explain why people opt for burial rather than cremation. While the buried ashes can be visited at the crematorium, for many bereaved people this is probably a poor substitute for visiting the grave, which at least once contained an intact body, and can be tended to as a way of 'taking care' of the deceased. It's also easier to leave flowers and other 'gifts' or tributes' at a graveside than at the crematorium. In Judaism, the erection of the headstone 12 months following the burial marks the official end of mourning, a major *rite de passage*.

THE MAKINGS OF A GOOD FUNERAL

The early 2000s saw a steady expansion in the types of funeral and options available. Both academic and popular commentators agree that funerals in late-modern Western societies reflect personalisation, secularisation, consumer choice, and individual stories.[27]

CONTRASTING THE MAJOR FEATURES OF TRADITIONAL AND POST-MODERN FUNERALS[28]

Traditional funerals commend the departed, symbolically mark their passing on, and acknowledge the individual's life within a wider existential frame for understanding life and death.

By contrast, *post-modern funerals* (often dubbed 'DIY funerals') serve the needs of the bereaved, celebrate the life lived, and take the form of personally customised tributes.

During the 1980s there was a reaction against the impersonal way in which many religious funerals were conducted and the meaninglessness of the Christian liturgy for the majority of mourners. However, the increasing popularity of 'DIY' celebratory funerals has itself been criticised, for example (i) the abandonment of the traditional ritual has left mourners unable to express or manage their grief; and (ii) contemporary ceremonies are spiritually barren and ignore the spiritual needs of diverse cultural groups who may be attending.

These changes in the nature of funerals have taken place in parallel with a growing debate regarding the nature and place of religion and spirituality in modern society. What's increasingly referred to as 'humanistic spirituality' emphasises personal expression, life-enhancement, and individually-customised meanings over handed-down, traditional religious belief systems, all of which may or may not involve belief in some external power or divine being.[29] Ironically, these seemingly *secular* practices may have become new forms of religiosity and spirituality.

Recent research indicates that the contemporary funeral is a *psycho-social-spiritual* event.[30] The funeral is an illogical act for rational people, yet it remains remarkably preserved in all societies. A *physical procedure* (disposal of the body) is encapsulated in a ritual *social process* (the funeral) which demands a *philosophical response* on the part of the individual regarding the relationship between life and death. The funeral is designed to help people find *meaning* at a time of existential challenge: what does it mean to be human? This provides the *spiritual* dimension of modern funerals: it is that *process* of meaning-seeking, creating, and taking which shapes personalised funerals. This is what makes for a 'good funeral'.[31]

DISENFRANCHISED GRIEF

As noted in Chapter 1, *disenfranchised grief* (DG) represents an important demonstration of the impact of other people and social norms on individuals' response to bereavement. Essentially, DG refers to an individual's grief that is *not validated* by others: the person isn't accorded the 'right' to grieve. The right to grieve is a matter of human dignity and a fundamental human right.[32]

THE SCOPE OF DG

Grief can be disenfranchised in five major ways:[33] *relationships, losses, grievers, circumstances of the death*, and *how individuals grieve*.

Relationships may be disenfranchised if they're non-traditional (e.g. homosexual or extra-marital); are thought not to be close enough (e.g. are not with spouses or first-degree relatives – parents and siblings); have remained unsuspected or secret; or are viewed as acceptable although their full implications are not appreciated (e.g. with friends, in-laws, work colleagues, or ex-spouses). While homophobia is still all-too common in Western countries, the introduction in the U.K. of civil partnerships (in 2004) and full married status (in 2014) has helped to 'reclassify' grief for a same-sex partner/spouse as legitimate (i.e. it has become enfranchised). This illustrates the dynamic nature of social influences on grief: the social context of grief is constantly changing.

Losses may be disenfranchised when there's a failure to recognise that a death has been experienced as a significant loss, as in the case of birth terminations (abortions), miscarriages (see Chapter 5), loss of body parts (e.g. amputations), loss of pets or companion animals, the psychological/social deaths of Alzheimer's sufferers, prisoner deaths, or deaths on the 'losing' side in a war.

Grievers may be disenfranchised when there's failure to acknowledge that certain groups are *capable* of grieving (e.g. young children, elderly people, and people with learning disabilities).

Circumstances of the death may be disenfranchised if they inhibit either seeking or receiving support from other people (e.g. suicides, deaths from AIDS or other stigmatised diseases, and deaths induced by excessive use of alcohol or other substances).

The ways in which individuals grieve may be disenfranchised when styles of experiencing and expressing grief clash with the experience of others (e.g. when *instrumental* grievers fail to show a strong affective response, *intuitive* grievers show excessive emotion, or culturally-engrained stoicism or wailing violate the grieving 'rules' of a given society; see Chapter 1).

CULTURAL ASPECTS OF DEATH AND DYING

The cultural dimension of death and grief has been studied by anthropologists for a long time: a community's rituals and beliefs facilitating the passage between life and death throw light on its beliefs and practices. For most of us, in our everyday activities, culture is 'invisible' precisely because it's all around us and is a major part of our assumptive world (see Chapter 3); it's as 'natural and unremarkable as the air we breathe or as the solid ground beneath our feet'.[34]

Culture (from the Latin 'to cultivate') has many connotations, but in the context of bereavement and grief, it has been used to refer to how a people or groups of people construe their world: culture provides the templates for how people represent their experience and is, thus, the basis for their actions.[35]

CULTURAL DEFINITIONS OF LOSS AND GRIEF

Across cultures, most people seem to grieve the loss of someone close. We shall now consider three major types of response to bereavement and mourning that have been identified by anthropologists.

BELIEF IN THE CONTINUATION OF THE DECEASED'S RELATIONSHIPS WITH THE LIVING BEYOND BODILY DEATH

While these continuing relationships may be viewed positively or negatively, a sense of the persisting presence of the dead person is socially sanctioned and appropriate behaviour prescribed. This is nowhere more dramatically demonstrated than in Japan where, in both the Buddhist and Shinto religions, there's a deep-seated respect for ancestors, who are normally referred to by terms used to designate divine beings and whose spirits can be recalled.

Mourning rituals are prescribed which encourage a continuing relationship with any deceased person: every family erects an altar in the living room, with a photograph of the deceased, the urn containing the ashes, flowers, water, rice, and other offerings. A widow's first duty after her husband's death is to build an altar, which she visits at least once daily to offer incense, to ask his advice, or share her feelings – positive and negative – with him. In this way, the relationship is maintained through his transformation from living man to revered ancestor.

THE BELIEF THAT THE BEREAVED ARE EXPECTED TO FEEL ANGRY WITH THOSE RESPONSIBLE FOR THE DEATH

In most non-Western communities, most deaths are untimely (i.e. they involve children, adolescents, and young adults): the more untimely the death is felt to be, the more likely someone is held to blame. Most cultures define whom it's appropriate to blame – commonly members of a nearby village or tribe, the self, or the deceased. In some societies, active expression of anger is an established part of the funeral rites (and may involve verbal or physical attacks on the deceased), in others this is forbidden. In some cases, directing anger against the self is not only permitted but prescribed; for example, Jewish widows in Morocco tear their flesh with their fingernails until they bleed.

PRESCRIBING A TIME WHEN MOURNING SHOULD END

Many societies prescribe customs which seem to have the effect of helping widows to remarry and resume an apparently normal married life; examples include practising a taboo on the name of the deceased, destroying or disposing of his property, and changing residence. 'Officially' some of these customs may relate to fear of ghosts or contamination, but their true purpose is to impel a widow through the transition from widowhood to a new married life.[36]

IS THERE REALLY A DISTINCTION BETWEEN GRIEF AND MOURNING?

While these three responses to bereavement represent what different cultures have in common, there are also important differences in how they define death and appropriate expressions of grief. Indeed, we cannot experience our world outside the cultural framework we bring to it.[37] This implies that the distinction between grief as an internal, subjective process and mourning as its social expression is false (see Chapter 1).

The moment grief is expressed, it becomes mourning: death can only be experienced within a cultural context and grief can only be felt and expressed within cultural guidelines and expectations.[38]

Similarly, culture is such a crucial part of the context of bereavement that it's often impossible to separate an individual's grief from culturally required mourning. For example, in cultures with a belief system that says 'do not grieve because the deceased has gone to a better life', it's difficult to assess accurately what seems to be muted grief: how do we distinguish where the cultural norm rules that demand muted grief end and 'real' grief begins? Similarly, when the rules say 'cry', how do we tell whether the crying is genuine or merely conformity with cultural expectations? This suggests that the grief/mourning distinction may be peculiar to Western culture.

Two other fundamental aspects of culture's influence on grief are (i) its policing of grief; and (ii) its effect on how grief is handled.[39]

CULTURE POLICES GRIEF

The popular mantra among bereavement counsellors that 'there is no right way to grieve' may be misleading: all cultures regulate their members' mourning, subtly or openly, implicitly or explicitly. *Individual grief narratives* (bereaved people's accounts or 'stories' of the death) are subjected to a *dominant grief narrative*.[40] Society controls and instructs the bereaved how to think, feel, and behave, and those who don't conform to social expectations are labelled as 'abnormal'.[41] In contemporary psychotherapeutic culture, abnormal grief is described as *complicated*, a term that largely replaced the former 'pathological' which made some bereavement counsellors uncomfortable (see Chapter 6).

POLICING GRIEF'S EMOTIONS

Cultures differ widely regarding which emotions are acceptable and how overtly they may be expressed, most clearly in relation to gender. For example, anthropological studies indicate where there are differences: women seem to cry and to attempt self-mutilation more than men; men seem to show more anger and aggression directed away from the self. This corresponds to the distinction between *intuitive* (female) and *instrumental* (male) grieving (see Chapter 1).

An important example of how *national character* may also play a part is the outpouring of grief following the death of Diana, Princess of Wales. While the Windsors followed the coffin showing almost none of the deeply conflicting feelings her death must have evoked, the public, for whom she was their 'queen of hearts', wept and embraced openly – a very 'un-British' expressiveness that seemed to contradict the 'stiff upper lip' stereotype.

POLICING CONTINUING BONDS

As we saw, Japanese widows maintain their relationship with their dead husband via the altar. The dead as a whole pass easily from one world to another; they are both 'here' and 'there'.

The mass slaughter of soldiers in the 1914–18 World War overwhelmed the Victorian ideal of maintaining sentimental attachment between the living and the dead; by the end of the war, grief was being regarded as a private, individual process with few social customs to support it. Pathological grief was now defined in terms of failure to relinquish the useless attachment to the deceased. Freud's 'grief work' theory was largely influenced by this mass killing, but the pendulum has swung back (since the mid-1990s) to the importance of maintaining bonds with the deceased (see Chapter 3).

CULTURE AFFECTS HOW GRIEF IS HANDLED

In terms of the dual process model (DPM)'s advocacy of a balance between loss-oriented and restoration-orientated coping, observations in China seem to indicate that there's recently been a disproportionate emphasis on *restoration*. Following the earthquake in Sichuan in 2008, tens of thousands of widows and widowers remarried shortly after their spouses' deaths. Also, a significant number of middle-aged mothers who lost their only child used reproductive technology to get pregnant soon afterwards.

Compared with U.S. participants, Chinese bereaved people have been shown to experience more acute distress in the first few months but a faster improvement thereafter. This relatively more 'efficient' way of grieving might be related to the cultural value of *pragmatism*, the idea of moving on with life, and participation in ancestor rituals that restrict overt grieving to specific prescribed dates.[42]

SUB-CULTURAL OR ETHNIC DIFFERENCES

Countries such as the U.S. and U.K. are culturally diverse ('multicultural'), which means that we cannot just assume that what is 'normal' for one individual or family will also be normal for others. There's a tendency to underestimate differences in relation to beliefs and practices regarding death and grief; this, in turn, may lead to intolerance and either failing to recognise the need of ethnic group members for emotional support or offering them an inappropriate form of support. For example, WASP (White Anglo-Saxon Protestant) Americans (and British) tend to 'psychologise' their emotional pain, while people in many other ethnic groups tend to 'somatise' theirs[43] (see Chapter 1). Hence, WASP people may find it difficult to support non-WASP-like grief.

Each of the three themes explored above (culture's policing of grief, its affect on how grief is handled, and sub-cultural/ethnic differences) have implications for practice. For example, the striving for balance between loss- and restoration-oriented coping as recommended by the DPM may not be equally appropriate for all cultural/sub-cultural (or ethnic) groups. Also, in addition to the primary loss of the loved one, the bereaved person may need support in dealing with the *secondary stressors* induced by how family and friends are judging the (in)appropriateness of his/her grieving. Theories of grief and the techniques used to help the bereaved are themselves as culture-bound as any other aspect of bereavement.[44]

5

GRIEF AND OUR
RELATIONSHIP
TO THE DECEASED
WHO HAS DIED?

While both the experience and expression of grief are shaped by social and cultural influences, bereaved individuals within the same socio-cultural group still vary enormously in how they respond to the loss of a loved one. In turn, who that loved one is (or was) will help determine the nature and intensity of their grief response.

In this chapter, 'relationship to the deceased' denotes kinship, i.e. how they were (genetically or legally) related (e.g. spouse, child, parent, sibling). By contrast, in Chapter 3 we discussed attachment theory as a way of evaluating our relationships with others, (i.e. secure/insecure) in particular, children's attachments to their parents and spouses' attachments to each other. Both kinship and the strength and security of attachment represent 'risk factors' for complicated grief (see Chapter 6).

SPOUSAL BEREAVEMENT: THE LOSS OF A HUSBAND, WIFE, OR PARTNER

Most of the research into the prediction of risk after bereavement has been conducted with widows and widowers in the English-speaking world: it represents a kind of 'default option'.

As noted in Chapter 1, a number of the earlier studies of bereavement involved widows (and sometimes widowers as well). It's also important to point out that the dual process model (DPM), arguably the most influential and oft-cited of all major theories/models of grief, was originally developed with widowhood in mind.

This focus on widow(er)s is partly a reflection of its frequency and inevitability (it's 'on-time'). Especially in later life, spousal bereavement is a high probability event for women, who are likely to outlive their husbands/male partners and who tend to marry or partner men older than themselves in the first place. This, combined with the fact that widowed men are more likely to remarry than women, means that men don't expect to be widowers as much as women expect to be widows. Also, cultural norms encourage men to marry women younger than themselves, so widowed men may opt to remarry younger women; older widows don't typically have access to a similarly expanded pool of potential spouses.[1]

SPOUSAL BEREAVEMENT VERSUS WIDOW(ER) HOOD

As a general rule, the loss of a spouse affects almost every domain of life, and as a consequence has a significant impact on psychological, social, physical, practical, and economic well-being[2] (i.e. the *secondary* losses that are part of the fall-out of the bereavement [the *primary* loss]; see Chapters 1 and 3).

The terms 'spousal bereavement' and 'widowhood' are often used interchangeably, both in everyday conversation and by researchers and practitioners. However, while *spousal bereavement* is the state of having experienced the death of one's spouse, with (usually) short-term *personal* consequences and meanings, *widowhood* is a long-term, ongoing state which has both personal and *social* consequences and meanings (see Chapter 4).

For example, short-term disruptions to sleeping and eating patterns are quite a common consequence of bereavement (see Chapter 1), which don't often continue into long-term widowed life; two years is often regarded as an appropriate cut-off point for 'normal' grieving (see Chapter 6) or these 'symptoms' may not be seen as related to the bereavement at all. Longer-term consequences – more likely to be associated with the state of widowhood – include continuing changes in identity (which demonstrate the interaction between the intra- and interpersonal) and changes in friendships, social support, and status. Widowed women in particular talk about changes in their friendships, how they are dropped by their married friends and make new friendships with other widows. They also speak of how little social support (formal or informal) they receive compared with their widower friends. Men also face a reduced social network when their wife dies, and remarrying is one solution to this problem.[3]

Another illustration of the normative nature of spousal bereavement (i.e. it's both common and expected) is the history of Cruse Bereavement Care, the U.K.'s largest provider of bereavement support.

A BRIEF HISTORY OF CRUSE BEREAVEMENT CARE

Cruse began life in 1959 in the home of Margaret Torrie, a Quaker with a social work background, as a pilot scheme: a small group of widows in Richmond, Surrey, met to discuss the needs and problems created by widowhood – and society's attitude to bereavement. It was subsequently launched as a National Charity, with local branches where committees could be formed.

In 1970, Torrie published Begin Again: A Book for Women Alone, which became the 'bible' for widows (especially the young and middle-aged), social workers, relatives, and so on. In 1972, Parkes's Bereavement: Studies of Grief in Adult Life gave bereavement a much higher profile. He is Cruse's first Life President (since 1992) and was awarded the OBE for his services to bereaved people in 1996.

In 1974, Cruse received its first government grant as recognition of its valuable community work and in the field of preventative healthcare. In 1980, widowers were formally included within Cruse's provision of help and changed its name to 'Cruse: The National

Organisation for the Widowed and their Children'. It was formally decided to extend provision to *all* bereaved people in 1986. The name 'Cruse Bereavement Care' was adopted in 1987.

Spousal loss is the most frequent type of bereavement leading to psychiatric referral.[4] Among the factors which have been shown to predict problematic reactions to the death of a partner in several studies are an ambivalent or dependent relationship. For example, in Parkes's Love and Loss Study (see Chapter 1), people who were referred for psychiatric help following the death of a partner were, on average, older and more often left to live alone than those referred following other kinds of loss. Both men and women reported significantly higher rates of unusual closeness to, and dependence on, their partners, less aggression and assertiveness, and greater loneliness after the partner's death; this loneliness was not reduced either by living with others or having a confidant(e). As a group, these widowed individuals were intensely bound up with their partner in a passive and mutually dependent way. The attachment to the deceased partner was *exclusive* and no substitute for a lost partner was acceptable.

SPOUSAL BEREAVEMENT AS NORMATIVE AND NON-NORMATIVE

As noted earlier, for the majority of older widowed people widowhood is a common experience, with common and familiar effects. For example, some studies have shown that the widowed experience lower levels of psychological well-being, higher levels of depressive symptoms, lower morale, and reduced social engagement four to eight years following bereavement. However, other studies suggest that the negative impact of becoming widowed on psychological health may recover over time.

As far as physical health is concerned, the picture is less straightforward. A number of researchers have suggested that it is health *behaviours* and health *maintenance* behaviours which are challenged by bereavement. For example, widows may eat less well, sleep patterns may be disrupted, and consulting the GP may increase or decrease;

these changes may depend on who was the health 'gatekeeper' – traditionally, the wife – and whether s/he is the one who has died. Men in particular are more likely to die themselves, from a wide range of causes, but particularly from accidents; there's also evidence of people dying from a broken heart.

For younger widowed people, bereavement is a *non-normative* event and is associated with a greater decline in physical and psychological health. Off-time widowhood is seen as the most disruptive because younger adults are generally less prepared emotionally and practically than older adults to cope with spousal loss. Symptoms are both more severe and pronounced when the death is sudden and unexpected (see Chapter 6). Becoming a single parent is one of the major secondary losses associated with becoming widowed at an early age.

SPOUSAL BEREAVEMENT IN LATER LIFE

Adjustment to bereavement can be affected by a wide range of biological, psychological, social, and economic factors. Recent research has identified four particularly important influences: (i) the nature of the relationship; (ii) circumstances surrounding the death; (iii) social support and integration; and (iv) other co-occurring losses and stressors.[5]

NATURE OF THE RELATIONSHIP

Those writing from a psychoanalytic perspective (i.e. based on Freud's theories) predicted that bereaved people with the most troubled marriages would suffer heightened and pathological grief: they would find it hard to let go of their spouse, but at the same time feel angry at the deceased for having abandoned them. However, longitudinal studies that track married couples over time and into the widowhood transition have found the *opposite* to be true: older people whose marriages were warm and mutually dependent, with little conflict, experience *heightened* levels of grief within the first six months post-loss.

However, the strong emotional ties to the deceased spouse may prove *protective* in the longer term (see the discussion of Continuing

Bonds in Chapter 3). Maintaining a psychological tie to the deceased is an integral part of adaptation, as when the bereaved partner wonders what the late spouse would have done in a challenging situation that s/he has to face. Others may keep the late spouse's legacy alive by recognising the continuing positive influence the deceased has on one's current life.

CIRCUMSTANCES SURROUNDING THE DEATH

In general, anticipated deaths tend to be less distressing than unanticipated ones: knowing that one's partner is going to die imminently gives the couple time to address unresolved emotional, financial, and practical issues before the actual death; this preparation for death makes the transition to widowhood smoother. However, for older people, 'anticipated' deaths are often accompanied by long-term illness, painful images of the loved-one's suffering, intensive caregiving, and neglect of one's own health; this can all take a toll on the survivor's physical health and emotional well-being.

Yet some research suggests that caregivers' psychological health may actually improve following the loss because they are relieved of their burden of stressful caregiving duties: they no longer have to witness their loved one suffer, or they experience a sense of satisfaction from caring for their partner in his/her final days.

Use of hospice/palliative care services (including hospice-at-home care) is associated with better bereavement outcomes as compared with hospital or nursing home. The former is seen as offering high-quality care, dignity and respect, and adequate emotional support, all contributing to a 'good death'. However, as we saw in Chapter 4, most people in Western countries will die in a hospital.

SOCIAL SUPPORT AND INTEGRATION

Women's emotionally intimate social relationships during their lifetime are an important resource as they adjust to widowhood. Older widows typically receive more practical and emotional support from their children than do widowers, reflecting mothers' closer relationships with their children. Women are also more likely to have larger and more varied friendship networks than men, and these represent an important source of support as women cope with their loss. As noted earlier, men are more likely to seek social support through new romantic relationships (whether dating or remarriage).

OTHER LOSSES AND STRESSORS

For older bereaved persons, the death of a spouse is almost always accompanied by other losses and stressors which may compromise their well-being, including financial difficulties, the loss of work and community roles (including retirement and relocation), compromised mobility, health deterioration, worsening of sight and vision, and even the loss of daily routines that gave life order and meaning.

These losses and stressors are *additional* to the *secondary* losses resulting from the bereavement itself; these may also compromise emotional and physical well-being. For widowers, the loss of a confidante, helpmate, and caregiver may be particularly harmful, while for widows, financial and practical difficulties are often a major source of distress. Because the current generation of older women typically have had fewer years of paid work, they will have smaller pensions compared with older widowers.

LOSS OF A PARENT IN ADULT LIFE

'Most people who reach the age of 50 are orphans; they will have lost one or both parents'.[6] Despite spousal bereavement being the normative loss as far as the major theories/models of grief are concerned, the largest group of people going to Cruse Bereavement Care in 2013–2014 were those who'd experienced the death of a parent.[7] This is consistent with statistics for previous years.

Most studies of the psychological effects of the loss of a parent have involved children of school or pre-school age, when the death of a parent is relatively uncommon. In general, it appears that in this age group long-term problems are more likely to arise from inadequate subsequent parental care than from the loss itself (yet another example of the impact of *secondary* losses).

LOSS OF PARENTS IN YOUNG ADULTHOOD

Because loss of one's parents as an adult is *normative* and timely, there are few studies of its effects compared with the number of child studies.[8] However, there has, traditionally, been an even greater dearth of studies of the effects of parental loss when children are in their teens and early-mid 20s; clearly, losing a parent at this age is *not* normative and timely.[9]

If the death is also sudden (as in a fatal heart attack), there's no opportunity to prepare, which 'leaves you feeling that the whole world has become an unsafe and unreliable place in which nothing can be trusted or valued any longer'.[10] Perhaps the hardest aspect of a parent's death for young people – and the most consistently overlooked and misunderstood – is that grief involves feelings of helplessness and lack of control that are exceptionally difficult to cope with when you're at precisely the stage of your life when you need to feel in control and taking charge of your life: this might make grieving *impossible*, postponing it until sometimes 20 or more years later. One implication of this is that, in order to understand a person's grief and to be able to support him/her through it, it's necessary to *contextualise* it within his/her life at the time the bereavement occurred.

Compared with previous generations, many more young people will still be living at home (either never having left or having returned) when one of their parents dies. Also, with *blended* families fast becoming the norm (see Chapter 4), young people are much more likely than in previous generations to experience the deaths of both biological and step-parents (as well as step-siblings and other step-relatives).

DEATH OF AN ELDERLY PARENT

While adult children begin to prepare for the deaths of elderly parents and to see these as normative occurrences, there's no consensus as to whether such anticipation mitigates the impact of the loss.[11] In cases of dementia (such as Alzheimer's disease), the loss seems to occur *before* death itself and has appropriately been called *ambiguous* (see Chapter 1). Adult children who've been caring for their sick parent may experience a range of responses to his/her death: sorrow, clinical depression, numbness, relief, and guilt, and emotional distress increase for those who were already distressed prior to the death. Dementia only serves to highlight a more general phenomenon: old people often become physically and emotionally dependent on their children, which can re-arouse earlier attachment problems and spoil the final years together.

As parents become old, their adult children begin to display signs of *adaptation anxiety*,[12] such as worrying about how to provide for parents at the very end of life, how to cope with their actual dying, and how to manage their life without them. The evidence is mixed regarding the benefits of anticipatory grieving; for example, an anticipated death that's difficult and drawn out over a protracted period of time may have severe psychological costs – especially if the parent experienced significant suffering.

In the main, complicated or pathological grief is rare for surviving adult children; however, increased rates of depression and even suicide have been reported. This increase in suicide was largely confined to men who'd never married and continued to live with their mother.[13] A minority of adult children may not have fully achieved the autonomy (usually during adolescence) which allows us to survive without our parents' nurture. Unusually close attachments may persist, reducing the chance of making new relationships and spoiling those that are made. When the parent finally dies, this may threaten mental health; on the other hand, it may also provide the orphans with opportunities to discover their true worth, strength, and potential.[14]

Because women marry men who, on average, are older than themselves, and because men, on average, die earlier than women, most people lose their father before their mother. It could be that the greater distress expressed following a mother's death reflects the fact that she will have been the remaining parent and so the adult child is now parent-less (a 'true' orphan); the child has now moved to the 'head of the queue' (unless there's an older sibling or siblings; see the next section). 'There is nothing like the death of a parent to bring home the prospect of one's own mortality'.[15]

LOSS OF A SIBLING IN CHILDREN AND ADULTS

> Our relationships with our siblings are the longest-lasting we'll probably have – longer than those with our parents or partners, or with our children. Indeed, towards the end of the lifespan, relationships between siblings take on particular importance for many people as sources of support.[16]

Consequently, the death of a brother or sister can be traumatic for siblings at any age; indeed, siblings' stories reveal that the impact of such a death lasts a lifetime, influencing their surviving siblings' ways of being in the world. While the impact of sibling death in childhood is well documented, this isn't the case in adulthood.

CHILDHOOD SIBLING LOSS

Many factors affect children's grief responses to a sibling's death, including the child's age and gender, health status, temperament or coping style, previous experience with loss, cause and location of death, duration of the sibling's illness, and the degree to which they were involved in the sibling's illness and events surrounding the death (such as the funeral or memorial service).[17] Bereaved children who are actively involved in the care of their sibling or in planning the funeral or related events display fewer behavioural problems than those who are excluded. Giving children a clearly informed choice about whether or not they want to be involved is of key importance.

Also critical is the nature of the pre-death relationship. When siblings have shared many aspects of their lives, the loss of one of them leaves a large empty space in the surviving sibling(s).

SIBLING BEREAVEMENT RESPONSES

Both children and adolescents have been found to respond to the death of a sibling in four characteristic ways.[18]

'I HURT INSIDE'

This includes all the physical responses and emotions typically associated with grief that arise from the vulnerability of being human, from loving others and missing them when they're no longer with us (see Chapter 2). Unlike adults, children are often unable or inexperienced at identifying what they're feeling; instead, they express emotions through behaviour. This can take many forms, some quite clearly signs of grief (such as eating and sleeping disturbances), and others not (such as decline in school performance).

'I DON'T UNDERSTAND'

How children begin to make sense of death depends on their level of cognitive development; once they have personal experience of death, their worlds are changed forever. As they develop new ways of understanding and approaching the world, they will have new questions about the death and will want to hear the story of the death afresh.

'I DON'T BELONG'

A death in the family tears apart the normal day-to-day patterns of family life. Parents are overwhelmed by their grief and siblings don't know what to do or how to help (or if they should try); they may begin to feel as if they're not part of what's happening. Over time, as roles and responsibilities realign within the family, siblings may feel as if there's no longer a place for them.

'I'M NOT ENOUGH'

Siblings typically want to help reduce their parents' despair, but nothing they do seems to help, and they may begin to feel they're 'not enough' to make their parents happy. Moreover, some may feel that the deceased sibling was the parents' favourite: they should have been the one to die. These feelings can be exacerbated if the mother subsequently has another child (see the earlier discussion of loss of a parent in young adulthood).

These responses also apply to adults who have lost a sibling in childhood.

ADULT SIBLING LOSS

Echoing many aspects of the descriptions given of the sibling's grief responses, it has been observed that:

> There are the efforts, often lifelong, to preserve the dead sibling in some way, and the efforts to save others in the way the living sibling should have saved the dead sibling. For many children . . . the only solution is to become especially good.[19]

J.M. Barrie, who immortalised his brother, David, in *Peter Pan*, the boy who would never grow up, is a case in point. David was killed in a skating accident, aged 13, when Barrie was aged six. This immortalisation through literature is an extreme example of trying to keep the deceased alive through our memories of them (see discussion of Continuing Bonds in Chapter 3).

The adult sibling tie helps to connect this discussion of sibling loss with the earlier discussion of loss of one's parents in adulthood.[20] When elderly parents die, many adult children are shocked by the discovery that they're now facing the world 'on their own' – despite feeling prepared for this normative death. Some people stay close to their siblings, even though they may not particularly like them, because they feel that the connection to their siblings maintains the connection to their deceased parents who, somehow, continue to act as a buffer between themselves and the infinite.[21]

Sibling loss has been described as a *disenfranchised loss* (see Chapter 4): friends, work colleagues, and even relatives are often ill-prepared to offer support and simply don't understand the pain. This lack of support is mirrored by their own failure to grasp their loss: losing a sibling isn't seen as normative or part of the 'natural order', unlike the loss of elderly parents. At the same time, they may have to support their elderly grieving parents who have lost a child. In addition, the relationship with the deceased sibling's family (sister- or brother-in-law and nieces and nephews) is changed.

THE LOSS OF A CHILD

The loss of a child will always be painful, for it is in some way a loss of part of the self. . . . In any society, the death of a young child seems to represent some failure of family or society and some loss of hope.[22]

Regardless of the age of the child, 'to most people in the West, the death of a child is the most agonising and distressing source of grief'.[23] While we might expect the loss of a baby or young child to be the most painful of all, the loss of an adult child appears to result in more intense, or more persistent, grief and depression than loss of a spouse, parent, or sibling.[24]

However, in Third World countries, women continue to have large families because they expect many of their children to die; here the death of a child, especially in infancy, is *less* psychologically devastating than it is in Western countries. In the Western 'medically privileged world', a child's death is untimely and non-normative, and is often traumatic, sudden, and sometimes inexplicable (as in sudden infant death syndrome/SIDS, discussed later in this chapter).[25]

Inevitably, when a child dies, and however it dies, parents will feel cheated of the child's life and future. Their relationship with their child begins long before birth and each parent has a fantasy child, built on the pre-conception images of what a baby – this baby – will be. Many pregnancies are unplanned or unwanted (initially or even throughout), making the relationship with the unborn baby highly ambivalent.[26] However, the loss of a baby will always need to be grieved for, at whatever stage of pregnancy this might occur.

MISCARRIAGE (SPONTANEOUS ABORTION)

The level of the mother's grief will be affected by whether or not the baby was wanted; this can be true even with an early miscarriage (i.e. before the baby is viable).[27] But after the baby's movements have been felt, it's more likely to be seen as the loss of a 'person': the loss isn't 'nothing' or 'just a scrape' (dilatation and curettage), but the beginning of a baby. The use of technical terms to describe the baby – 'conceptus', 'embryo', 'foetus' – might be perceived as an attempt to deny the existence of a baby the woman already loved, and thus to deny the reality of the grief she experiences for that baby.[28]

TERMINATION (THERAPEUTIC OR INDUCED ABORTION)

In the U.K., the 1990 Abortion Act makes it possible for a woman to have an abortion legally up to 24 weeks of pregnancy, provided two doctors independently agree that the termination was necessary to prevent the likelihood of the woman's death, permanent illness (physical or psychological), damage to a woman's existing children, or abnormality in the baby.

Despite its legality, abortion is still a very much debated moral issue. Many authors have proposed that abortion may have adverse mental health effects owing to guilt, unresolved loss, and lowered self-esteem. The pattern of grief is similar to that for miscarriage, but suppression or inhibition of grief is much more likely.

STILLBIRTH

A stillbirth occurs when a baby born after 24 weeks' gestation fails to breathe. Knowledge of the fact that there's no live baby at the end of the labour can magnify the experience of pain. The unusual nature of this type of death marks parents out as 'different': it is stigmatising. However, for some parents there may be positives to be found in their loss (see Chapter 7).

Over the past 40 years, understanding of stillbirth and its effect on parents has changed markedly. For example, Sands (The Stillbirth and Neonatal Death Charity), formed in 1978 by bereaved parents angry at the lack of recognition of their loss, has made important progress working with health professionals and publication of guidelines. Sands recommends that parents be offered the chance to see, hold, and spend time with their baby, and many hospitals now have a bereavement midwife and other specially trained staff.

SUDDEN INFANT DEATH SYNDROME (SIDS)

SIDS refers to the unexpected and abrupt death of an infant under 12 months old (also called *cot death* in the U.K. and *crib death* in the U.S.).[29] It accounts for more deaths of infants between 1 and 12 months than any other cause, with a peak between 2 and 4 months.

Apart from violation of the general 'rule' that parents shouldn't outlive their children (of whatever age), three prevalent emotional responses to a SIDS death are extreme guilt, anger, and blame; also, communication between spouses and mutual emotional support decline (see the next section).

Mothers and fathers display discrepant coping responses and 'dyssynchronous patterns of recovery'. Consistent with the gender-related distinction between intuitive and instrumental grief (see Chapter 1), mothers tend to be more depressed, withdrawn, and more disrupted by their loss, while fathers take over protective, management functions, suppress their feelings, and cannot understand their wives' continuing preoccupation with the death. Fathers' responses are also angrier and more aggressive than the mothers'.[30] This mirrors the response to stillbirth.

Given that the cause of SIDS is still unknown, parents' dread that they are powerless to prevent such a tragedy occurring again is increased. It's as though caring for their infant was futile, which does nothing to assuage their overwhelming guilt and self-blame.[31] Not surprisingly, SIDS constitutes a risk for complicated grief[32] (see Chapter 6).

CHANGES IN THE COUPLE RELATIONSHIP FOLLOWING LOSS OF A CHILD

Bereaved couples are left to negotiate the challenge of fostering mutually supportive relationships while dealing with their own grief. While supportive families can serve to buffer or protect the bereaved couple, this isn't always forthcoming (as in stillbirth and other *disenfranchised* grief responses). Without such support, the death of a child can have a profoundly negative effect on the quality of the couple's relationship.

The section below describes some of the *metaphors* used by male and female partners following the death of a child; these metaphors can help the bereaved to describe and express their grief, the negotiation of the grief process with their partner, as well as the nature of the relationships left behind. Metaphors represent 'the lens through which they conceptualise their relationships'[33] (see the discussion of metaphors in Chapter 2).

RELATIONAL METAPHORS FOLLOWING THE DEATH OF A CHILD[34]

In an online survey, 420 bereaved parents, mainly white, well-educated females, on average just over four years since their bereavement, were asked: 'In your own words, please tell us how your loss affected your relationship with your spouse or partner'. Three major themes emerged from the metaphors used by the participants.

Of those who responded, 71.5 per cent said that the child's death had brought them closer together (e.g. 'strengthened our marriage'), 20.8 per cent said that it had pushed them apart (e.g. 'it nearly destroyed us'), and 7.7 per cent said that their relationship had periods of strain and coming together (e.g. 'tear us apart or make us stronger').

Grief in relation to a partner was commonly described in terms of enduring a difficult journey (see Chapter 2). Understanding and adapting to a partner's different grieving style proved challenging for many, as reflected in being on different paths. While some were able to adjust to these differences and accept them for what they were, for others the difference was too great, as illustrated by 'He could not take that I cried and he eventually left'.

The decision about whether or not to discuss the topic of the death was metaphorically reflected by several participants as 'the elephant in the room' or 'we tiptoed around the issue'. For most, effective communication between couples was metaphorically described as 'open'.

PARENTING CHALLENGES AFTER THE DEATH OF A CHILD

As noted in the discussion of children's responses to the loss of a sibling, children also often experience a significant change in their relationship with their grieving parents. Turning that around, many bereaved parents must also contend with the challenges of parenting their surviving, bereft children.[35]

Surviving siblings suffer many secondary losses in the form of their parents' functional incapacity and the demise of the comforting safety, security, and predictability their family previously provided. Bereaved parents are confronted with the 'delicate, complicated task of simultaneously relinquishing their parental role with their deceased child while continuing to function in this capacity with surviving children'.[36]

This *bereaved parenting* is a complex and intimidating task that involves a number of themes. These include: (i) responding to loss-induced personality and behaviour changes in their surviving children; (ii) revisiting the loss over time: the death is reviewed as bereaved siblings mature and can accommodate a deeper understanding of the loss and its profound impact; (iii) appreciating and adjusting to their children's differing grieving styles: where there is more than one surviving child, parents face the daunting task of differentially responding to each child's reaction to multiple levels of loss (e.g. loss of a friend, rival, confidant, playmate, and/or role model; the 'loss' of their parents in a functional sense; and the loss of their family as they knew it); (iv) enduring the powerlessness of being incapable of shielding their surviving children from such horrendous life experiences and the unavoidable pain of grief; and (v) helping the surviving sibling(s) to make sense of a meaningless, incomprehensible, and tragic event while struggling to make sense of it themselves.

6

WHEN DOES GRIEF BECOME COMPLICATED?

Probably the most logical place to begin trying to understand complicated (problematic, 'abnormal', or pathological) grief is to remind ourselves of what major theories and models tell us about uncomplicated ('normal') grief. As we saw in Chapters 2 and 3, these models and theories present accounts of what normal or healthy grieving *should* look like, be it withdrawing emotional energy from the deceased;[1] *stages* that need to be gone through (though not necessarily in a fixed, rigid, order);[2,3] *tasks* that need to be accomplished and completed;[4] *oscillating* between *loss*-orientation and *restoration*-orientation;[5] adapting to change and creating a new assumptive world;[6] or maintaining emotional bonds with the deceased.[7]

GRIEF WORK AND COMPLICATED GRIEF

In most of the accounts mentioned in the previous paragraph, the focus is on healthy grieving, with the nature of abnormal or complicated grief being implicit. However, Freud's psychoanalytic account of *grief work* states very clearly that pathological grief involves a failure to confront the reality of the death and psychologically let go of the deceased.

As noted in Chapter 3, many of the more recent models and theories (notably the dual process model [DPM] and Continuing Bonds) represent direct challenges to the grief work concept. We also noted that one of the major limitations of stage/phase models and Worden's task approach – which embody the grief work concept – is that they propose a 'one-size-fits-all' view of grief. We saw how research has shown how these traditional models have underestimated people's resilience in the face of loss.[8] Many normal grievers will adapt well to bereavement over the course of several months, with or without formal grief counselling – especially following more normative losses such as the death of a partner/spouse in later life.[9]

Similarly, the Continuing Bonds perspective claims that establishing ongoing emotional ties with the deceased is both healthier and more normative across human cultures than the notion of detachment from the deceased.[10] Evidence suggests that maintaining an emotional tie with the loved one may be comforting or distressing, depending on such factors as how far along survivors are in their bereavement, whether they've been able to make sense of the loss, and perhaps their level of security in important current attachments.

THE DPM, ATTACHMENT THEORY, AND COMPLICATED GRIEF

The DPM depicts grieving as a *cyclical* rather than linear and stage-like process, with the mourner repeatedly revisiting the loss and its associated emotions, striving to reorganise the relationship to the deceased, and taking on new roles and responsibilities necessitated by a changed world. This view of normal grieving also extends our understanding of pathological grieving, by suggesting that the inability to distract oneself from or avoid grief may be as much a sign of abnormality as the inability to confront it. However, we still cannot say exactly what constitutes the optimal balance and timing of focusing on the loss- and restoration-orientations.[11]

The DPM provides a framework for understanding complicated or pathological forms of grief (such as *chronic, absent, or inhibited*). In both loss-oriented (e.g. chronic) and restoration-oriented (e.g. absent) types of complicated grief, *reactions are extreme*, focusing excessively on one orientation and avoiding the other. This *disturbed oscillation* is *very* different from the confrontation-avoidance oscillation characteristic of 'normal' grieving.[12]

As noted in Chapter 3, the DPM predicts that the extent to which bereaved individuals will engage in either loss-oriented or restoration-oriented processes depends on various factors, in particular their attachment styles. *Securely attached* individuals would be expected to display healthy oscillation between loss- and restoration-related activities. *Anxious-avoidant* individuals would suppress and avoid attachment-related emotions and present absent or inhibited grief reactions, behaving as if nothing had happened and focusing on restoration-related activities. The bond with the deceased would be too *loose*.[13]

Anxious-ambivalent individuals would focus on the loss-orientation to the exclusion of restoration-related activities (i.e. chronic grief). The bond with the deceased would be too *strong*.[14] Finally, *disorganised* individuals would be unable to think and talk coherently about attachment-related memories and would show *traumatic grief* reactions.[15]

Anxiously-attached individuals have been described as *hyperaroused* (i.e. *over*-aroused) and avoidantly-attached individuals as *hypoaraoused* (i.e. *under*-aroused).

A MEANING RECONSTRUCTION APPROACH TO GRIEF

According to the *meaning reconstruction* approach to grief, bereavement challenges the survivor's self-narrative, the basic organisation of life events and themes that allows us to interpret the past, invest in the present, and anticipate the future.[16] The meaning systems people rely on to negotiate life transitions are often resilient, providing resources that help them to adapt. However, a painful search for meaning in the near aftermath of bereavement predicts more intense grief months and years later; by contrast, the capacity to find significance in the loss predicts greater long-term well-being and resilience (see Chapter 7).

This quest for meaning may be especially critical in cases of traumatic loss, such as – and perhaps especially – suicide (see pages 95–97), murder/homicide, and fatal accidents. An inability to make sense of these violent, unnatural deaths, appears to mediate their impact on the survivor's subsequent adaptation, perhaps especially in the case of suicide bereavement.[17] Similarly, studies of parents who have lost a child report that a struggle to make sense of the loss accounts for considerably more of the intensity of their grief compared with such objective factors as the passage of time, cause of death, or parents' gender[18] (see Chapter 5).

As we have noted at various points in earlier chapters, grieving – whether healthy or unhealthy, uncomplicated, or complicated – has traditionally been seen as something that takes place *within the individual*. However, recent approaches have begun to focus on the *transactional* nature of mourning at levels ranging from family processes to cultural discourses about bereavement. The meaning of the loss for an individual cannot be separated from the family, community, and societal meanings ascribed to death and loss and the resulting social responses to the mourner (see Chapter 5).

This more *systemic* approach recognises that the bereaved must adapt not only to a world where the deceased is no longer physically available, but also where the mourner's interactions with other people inevitably change: the latter approve or disapprove, support or don't support the mourner, acknowledge or don't the mourner's right to grieve (as in disenfranchised grief; see Chapter 4).

All these developments in bereavement theory are beginning to change our understanding of what constitutes a normal, expectable response to loss, and with it our view of what constitutes pathological grief.[19]

COMPLICATED GRIEF: SYMPTOMATOLOGY AND DIAGNOSIS

DIFFERENCES BETWEEN COMPLICATED AND UNCOMPLICATED GRIEF: QUANTITATIVE OR QUALITATIVE?

In general terms, complicated grief (CG) can be understood as something like a 'derailing' of the normal, usually painful process of adapting to the loss of a significant person.[20] Similarly, there's no sharp dichotomy between CG and uncomplicated grief (UCG): it's largely a matter of degree (i.e. there's only a *quantitative* difference between them).[21] For example, one view is that prolonged grief disorder (PGD) lies at one extreme end of a continuum, with 'normal', UCG, at the other (see next section).

However, at what point does a difference of degree become a difference of kind (i.e. a *qualitative* difference)? There's been much heated debate in recent years focusing on whether or not CG (specifically PGD) should be regarded – and treated – as a distinct mental disorder, that is, different from major depressive disorder (MDD), or post-traumatic stress disorder (PTSD). (CG is often described in terms that overlap with the symptoms of these 'well-established' mental disorders.)

PROLONGED GRIEF DISORDER (PGD)

Before 2013, the mental health community, as represented by the *Diagnostic and Statistical Manual of Mental Disorders* (DSM-IV-R, 2000; the 'bible' of American psychiatry, used throughout the world) didn't officially recognise any pattern of grief as pathological. Rather, bereavement was viewed as a life problem that, while it may sometimes need clinical attention, is not – in and of itself – a mental disorder. Any difficulties adjusting to a loss must be diagnosed in terms of depression, anxiety, or other disorders (such as PTSD).

However, a great deal of evidence has accumulated over the last 15 years or so that supports the diagnosis of 'CG' (which emphasises disruption of a normal grief 'journey') or 'PGD' (which stresses a chronic state of intense grieving that disturbs functioning over months or years). While these two terms are functionally equivalent, 'CG' is often used to highlight some grief response that differs from 'UCG' (or 'normal' grief), while PGD denotes a particular form that CG can take.

DIAGNOSTIC FEATURES OF PGD[22,23]

The major features of PGD (which need to have continued for at least six consecutive months) are (i) marked and persistent separation distress, reflected in intense feelings of loneliness, yearning for, or preoccupation with the deceased; and (ii) significant impairment in social, occupational, or family functioning (e.g. domestic responsibilities).

In addition, *at least five* of the following nine symptoms must have been experienced almost daily to a disabling degree: (i) diminished sense of self (e.g. self as empty or confused, or as if part of oneself has died); (ii) difficulty accepting the loss as real, both emotionally and intellectually; (iii) avoidance of reminders of the loss; (iv) inability to trust others or to feel that they understand; (v) extreme bitterness or anger over the death; (vi) extreme difficulty moving on with life (e.g. making new friends, pursuing new interests); (vii) pervasive numbness (absence of emotion/inability to feel) or detachment (social withdrawal); (viii) belief that life is empty and seeing the future as meaningless or without purpose; and (ix) feeling stunned, dazed, or shocked by the death.

The diagnosis of PGD refers to symptoms experienced by the bereaved person, regardless of the circumstances of the death (sudden/violent or not). A considerable amount of research has demonstrated that PGD is associated with increased rates of psychological distress, physical illness, and social dysfunction.

There have been several reports of an apparent relationship between bodily symptoms experienced by the bereaved person and those experienced by the dying spouse (or other loved one). Common examples include chest pains resembling the pain of coronary thrombosis, the apparent effects of a stroke, and recurrent (actual) vomiting. These are all examples of *identification symptoms*. In a few cases, the identification symptom is an exaggeration of symptoms that are common in 'normal' grief reactions (such as palpitations and gasping that often accompany anxiety but which 'mimic' a heart attack; see Chapter 1).

The features described in the preceding section have been shown to constitute a distinct symptom cluster, differing sufficiently from major depression (MDD) and post-traumatic disorder (PTSD) to be legitimately considered a separate diagnostic category (i.e. mental disorder).

IS THERE MORE TO CG THAN PGD?

While PGD may be a distinct mental disorder, we cannot simply equate CG with PGD. There are (at least) four different forms that CG can take,[24] one being *complicated grief symptoms*: The bereaved person experiences some psychological, behavioural, social, or physical symptoms of distress, disability, dysfunction, pathology, or loss of freedom. These symptoms represent a *compromise, distortion,* or *failure* in one/more of the normal grief processes.

Complicated grief syndromes represent a second form of CG. CG symptoms can combine to form one of seven CG syndromes: *absent* (or minimal); *delayed; inhibited; distorted* (of the extremely angry and guilty types); *conflicted; unanticipated;* and *chronic* (PGD is a type of chronic grief).

While minimal or absent grief reactions are very common, delayed grief reactions are quite rare; chronic grief/PGD has been generally well accepted as a pathological category. Chronic and absent grief have been well explained by the DPM (see pages 86–87). To the extent that unanticipated grief is associated with traumatic bereavement, it has been more extensively studied (see the discussion of suicide later in this chapter).

A third form of CG is *diagnosable mental or physical disorder*. Research consistently shows that bereavement can cause great suffering, associated with serious consequences for health and well-being. Bereaved individuals in general are at increased risk of physical and mental illness, in particular, depression and anxiety (see Chapter 1).

The fourth form of CG is *death*. This may be consciously chosen (i.e. suicide); research shows that CG is a risk factor for both *completed* suicide and *suicidality* (a tendency to attempt suicide). Also, death resulting from complicated grief-related behaviour can be 'sub-intended' or unintended, such as a car crash from drunk driving, or self-neglect.

RISK FACTORS FOR CG

Three of the six major categories of risk for CG are *kinship, gender and age,* and *personal responsibility*.[25] Much of the relevant research is discussed in Chapter 5 (also see Chapter 1). The loss of a spouse or child (especially to a violent, sudden death) has been found to be the most salient. Other important *potential* risk factors include being female and young, being a member of a minority group, having low levels of education, little income, and prior losses.[26] Relevant to personal vulnerability are different attachment styles (see Chapter 3) and related attachment disorders, high levels of pre-death marital dependency, and pre-existing psychological problems (such as disposition toward depression or anxiety). Also relevant here is the concept of *resilience* (see Chapter 2).

Other important risk factors include *social and cultural influences* (notably, lack of social support and low family cohesion; see later in this chapter and Chapter 4); *mode of death* (discussed later in this chapter); *multiple losses*, and *disenfranchised grief* (see Chapters 1 and 4).

CG AS A CULTURAL PHENOMENON

If we cannot properly understand UCG or 'normal' grief unless we examine it within its socio-cultural context, then the same applies to CG. However, the concept of CG and research on CG are grounded in a particular culture, and so we should be cautious about applying this to people of other cultures.[27] Also, to the extent that we all live in *pluralistic* (i.e. diverse, multicultural) societies, we should also be careful about applying the concept and clinical implications of CG to *all* people (or sub-cultural groups) within our own society.

In the U.S. and Europe, what's now seen as a problem (i.e. extreme, prolonged, intense grief) was at one time considered normal. In other words, norms regarding what is UCG or CG differ between different cultures and change over time within the same culture. Four major assumptions are commonly made in discussion of CG (in the main, by Western researchers), which should be made explicit.

ASSUMPTIONS REGARDING CG[28]

First, grief that goes on too long and too intensely is a problem that needs to be treated. (This is implicit in much of the chapter's preceding discussion about the nature of CG.) Second, judging that the grief has gone on for too long presupposes that there's a discrete point in time at which the loss can be said to occur; this point of time serves as a *marker* from which the duration of grieving can be measured. However, from a cross-cultural perspective, thinking of grief as arising at a discrete point in time is challenged by the experiences of people for whom a specific loss goes on continuously, occurs repeatedly, or is part of an ongoing series of losses. For example, there are several Native American cultures that have experienced severe historical traumas, including near-genocide, mass sexual abuse, and the destruction of culture and the social and physical environment, and these losses have been spread over many years and continue. In these cases, it would be a mistake to assume that grief can be assessed based on a discrete starting point.

Much of what's written about CG could be understood to imply that grieving in all cultures is essentially the same. However, there's considerable evidence that people deal with and talk about losses quite differently from one culture to another (see Chapter 4). Related to this is the concept of *recovery*, which is a concept of Western culture; in some cultures there may be no sense that something like recovery from grief is normal or desirable (see discussion of Tonkin's circles in Chapter 2).

Finally, looking at PGD, for example, as a *psychological* problem may lead us to ignore or discount what grieving people would say about their economic, political, or environmental challenges. Take the example of a Guatemalan widow whose husband has been assassinated by the military because he spoke out against injustices. Imagine that she continues to show symptoms of CG many years after his death and explains her pain largely in terms of the ongoing economic, political, and environmental oppression suffered by poor Guatemalans. If we suggest that she receives help to reduce the intensity of her grief, she may see this as a betrayal of crucial values. Her grief is being taken out of its context and so is being misunderstood.

THE MODE OF DEATH: CG AND TRAUMATIC BEREAVEMENT

Almost all those bereaved people who seek psychiatric help are found to have suffered unusually traumatic forms of bereavement and/or show evidence of prior vulnerability (see pages 91–92 and the following section).

> Sudden unexpected deaths, multiple deaths, violent deaths and deaths involving human agency (murders, suicides, etc.) represent a special risk to mental health even in the absence of other vulnerability.[29]

In most cases, death by natural causes is relatively untraumatic, although sudden unexpected deaths can, of course, be natural. 'Sudden unexpected' often – but not necessarily – implies *untimely*, as in any child death and those of teenagers and young adults.

SUDDEN/UNEXPECTED DEATHS

The young widows and widowers in the Harvard Study[30] were quite clearly more emotionally disturbed following deaths which they had little or no time to prepare for; their disturbance persisted throughout the first year of bereavement. 'Short duration of terminal illness' came first among 55 antecedent variables as a predictor of poor outcome 13 months after bereavement. Other American, as well as British and Swedish, studies have reported similar findings.

In young widows and widowers, the increased mortality that follows bereavement was greater after a sudden and unexpected death than if it was expected. While this was also found among older widowers – although to a lesser extent – there was no evidence of sudden death increasing mortality amongst older widows. The death of a spouse in old age may be sudden, but this doesn't mean that it's untimely.

Almost by definition, *sudden infant death syndrome* (SIDS) is likely to produce CG. Misunderstandings commonly arise in the course of police enquiries, parents may blame each other, and some engage in a relentless search for a cause. 'Shadow grief' may continue to plague some mothers every so often for the rest of their lives (see Chapter 5).[31]

A study of response to deaths of adult children in *road traffic accidents* found more intense grief in the bereaved parents (especially the mothers), more physical health problems, and greater depression and guilt compared with parents who had lost older adult children to cancer and who had died in hospice. The deaths of younger, unmarried children still living at home and of children killed in single-car, single-driver accidents, or who had alcohol or relationship problems, also predicted poor outcome in the parents.

VIOLENT DEATHS

These include murder and manslaughter, suicide, civil disaster, and military action, all of which have been shown to increase the risk of mental health problems. In cases of murder/manslaughter and suicide, anger and guilt are likely to predominate. The combination of sudden, unexpected, horrific, and untimely death, with all the rage and suspicions that follow, and the long, drawn-out legal proceedings, can overwhelm the family and lead to lasting psychological problems (such as PTSD and intense rage) and undermining trust in others.[32]

IS SUICIDE A SPECIAL CASE?

Whether, and in what ways, grief reactions to suicide are similar to or different from those produced by other causes of death has important implications for both research and the kind of support and clinical interventions they're offered.[33] A large number of empirical studies, clinical experience, and personal experience have helped identify the common features of the suicide-bereaved.[34] Typically, the suicide of a loved one increases levels of (one or more of) abandonment and rejection, shame and stigma, concealment of the cause of death as suicide, blaming, self-destructiveness or *suicidality*, guilt, anger, searching for an explanation/need to understand 'why' (meaning-making), relief, shock and disbelief, family system effects, social support issues, and/or social isolation, and activism, obsession with the phenomenon of suicide, and involvement with prevention efforts.

The suicide-bereaved are also more vulnerable to depression and psychiatric admission compared with those bereaved in other ways.[35] A framework for conceptualising differences between bereavement from suicide and other causes of death looks at the response to bereavement by suicide as incorporating: (i) *universal* or *normative* aspects (i.e. grief responses that apply to all bereavements, regardless of the cause of death); (ii) *non-normative* aspects (i.e. responses associated with all forms of *unexpected* and *sudden* death, as well as sudden, *violent* death); and (iii) responses that apply to all *traumatic* deaths.

While (i) describes very *general* aspects of grief, (ii) and (iii) describe increasingly *specific* aspects: the suicide-bereaved experience all those responses shared by *all* bereaved people (as described in Chapter 2), but *in addition* experience responses that are only associated with particular causes of death (sudden and violent, i.e. traumatic).

> Suicide bereavement is most different from mourning after death from natural causes; is somewhat different from other sudden, unexpected deaths; and is most similar to loss after other types of sudden and violent causes.[36]

But suicides aren't all the same; hence, their impact on the bereaved isn't always the same. Also, mode of death is only *one* variable that can affect the course and intensity of someone's grief.

SUICIDE AND GENDER

While more women worldwide attempt suicide (*parasuicide*) each year, more men actually die from suicide; for example, in the Western hemisphere, twice as many men complete suicide compared with women. While this gender gap has existed for at least 120 years, men now represent a large majority of all suicides across the world. Suicide is now the biggest single killer of young men in the U.K.

Until quite recently, the relationship between suicidal behaviour and men's gender has largely been taken for granted or marginalised. But the *construction of masculinities* is now believed to one of the most important factors influencing how men discuss, contemplate, and enact suicide. For example, male suicides are less likely than female suicides to have had contact with health services or to have been known to psychiatric services. This reflects the fact that men are less likely than women to consult for most conditions, especially mental health and emotional problems: men are supposed to deny pain, emotional sensitivity and anxiety, and asking for help, even in the face of possible suicide, may be viewed as feminine behaviour.[37]

Consistent with these 'masculinities' is the gender difference in how depression is *experienced*: while for women, the primary emotion is usually sadness, for men it's more typically anger or irritability, often coupled with recklessness. This is consistent with the typical instrumental and intuitive grieving styles of men and women, respectively (see Chapter 1).

7

THE POSITIVE SIDE OF GRIEF
POST-TRAUMATIC GROWTH

As far as we can tell, we are the only species that is aware of its mortality. Similarly:

> To a far greater extent than other animals, we as human beings are distinguished by living not only in a present, physical world, but also in a world populated by long-term memories, long-range anticipations, reflections, goals, interpretations, hopes, regrets, beliefs, and metaphors – in a word, *meanings*.[1]

However, there are occasions when the 'stubborn physicality of the present moment' threatens to or actually destroys our all-too-vulnerable *assumptive worlds* (see Chapter 3); such occasions include the diagnosis of our own serious illness and news of a loved one's sudden death.

> At such moments, we can feel cast into a world that is alien, unimaginable, and uninhabitable, one that radically shakes or severs those taken-for-granted 'realities' in which we are rooted, and on which we rely for a sense of secure purpose and connection.[2]

These moments are *crises of meaning*.[3]

Normally, we achieve a sense of identity through this meaning-making; specifically, we construct a life story (or *self-narrative*) that is uniquely our own, though it inevitably draws on the social discourses of our place and time (see Chapter 4). These self-narratives are the stories that we tell about ourselves and significant others. Importantly, it's precisely this self-narrative that is threatened and disturbed by 'seismic' life events such as the death of a loved one; they force us to reaffirm, repair, or replace the basic plot and theme of our life story.[4]

DIFFERENT LEVELS OF THE SEARCH FOR MEANING

In the aftermath of life-changing loss, the bereaved are commonly thrown into a *search for meaning*; this can take place at a *practical* level (*How* did my loved-one die?); a *relational* level (*Who* am I, now that I'm no longer a spouse?); or a *spiritual* or *existential* level (*Why* did God allow this to happen?).

How and whether we address these questions, and resolve or simply stop asking them, shapes how we accommodate the loss itself and who we become in the light of it.[5] However, loss doesn't inevitably destroy survivors' self-narratives: many people find consolation in systems of secular and spiritual beliefs and practices that have served them well in the past.[6] Especially when the death is normative and anticipated, only a minority of bereaved people report searching for meaning, and the absence of such a search is one predictor of a positive outcome.

MEANING, TRAUMATIC LOSS, AND COMPLICATED GRIEF

With regard to complicated grief, a struggle with meaninglessness is a critical marker of debilitating grief reactions such as prolonged grief disorder (PGD; see Chapter 6).[7] In the case of losses that are objectively more traumatic, trying to make sense of the loss is more common. Evidence shows that a crisis of meaning is especially acute for those bereaved by suicide, homicide, or fatal accident, compared with those whose loved ones die from natural causes. It's this need to make sense of the loss which accounts for almost all the difference between the complicated grief of those suffering a traumatic bereavement and the uncomplicated grief of those bereaved by natural causes.

Amongst a large group of parents who'd lost a child between a few months and several years previously, the passage of time, parent's gender, and even whether the child died a natural or violent death accounted for little of their subsequent adaptation: the degree of sense-making accounted for 15 *times more* of their distress than any of these objective factors.[8] The most common sense-making themes involved religious beliefs (e.g. their child's death was part of a divine plan, or a belief in reunion in the afterlife). However, a substantial proportion of these bereaved parents reported *benefits*, the most common benefit-finding themes involving an increased desire to help and show compassion for others' suffering. These benefits represented a renewed sense of hope and *self-efficacy* (i.e. the belief that one's actions will be effective and give us control over our lives). These parents experienced fewer maladaptive grief symptoms.

POST-TRAUMATIC GROWTH

An outcome such as an increased desire to help others is an example of *post-traumatic growth* (PTG). Various philosophies, literatures, and religions throughout history have claimed that personal gain can be found in suffering.[9] The concept of PTG denotes how trauma can serve as a catalyst for positive changes.[10] It stimulated considerable research interest and the study of PTG has become one of the flagship topics for positive psychology (PP).[11]

EVIDENCE FOR PTG

It's been found that 30–90 per cent of people who experience some form of traumatic event report at least some positive changes following the trauma (the figure varies according to the type of event and other factors).[12] A large number of studies have shown that growth is common for survivors of various traumatic events, including transportation accidents (shipping disasters, plane crashes, car accidents), natural disasters (hurricanes, earthquakes), interpersonal experiences (combat, rape, sexual assault, child abuse), medical problems (including cancer, heart attack, brain and spinal cord injury, HIV/AIDS), and other life experiences (relationship breakdown, parental divorce, bereavement). Typically, 30–70 per cent of survivors report positive change of one form or another.[13]

WHAT HAPPENS DURING PTG?

An interplay of several classes of variables is potentially central in the likelihood of PTG developing following trauma.[14] These variables include: cognitive processing, engagement, or rumination; expression or disclosure of concerns surrounding traumatic events; reactions of others to self-disclosures; the socio-cultural context in which traumas occur and attempts to process, disclose, and resolve take place; survivors' personal dispositions and the degree of resilience; and the degree to which events allow for these processes to occur, or the degree to which events suppress them.

HOW IS PSYCHOLOGICAL FUNCTIONING INCREASED?

Following the experience of a traumatic event, people often report particular ways in which their psychological functioning is enhanced:[15] (i) *relationships are enhanced in some way* (for example, people say they come to value their friends and family more, feel an increased sense of compassion for others, and a longing for more intimate relationships); (ii) *people change their view of themselves* (for example, they develop wisdom, personal strength, and gratitude, possibly combined with a greater acceptance of their vulnerabilities and limitations); and (iii) *people describe changes in their philosophy of life* (for example, they might find a fresh appreciation for each new day and re-evaluate their understanding of what really matters in life; this may manifest as becoming less materialistic and better able to live in the present. This re-setting of priorities involves identifying *core values*).

PTG involves the re-building of the shattered *assumptive world*. Instead of trying to put their lives back together as they were before the trauma, 'those who accept the breakage and build themselves anew become more resilient and open to new ways of living'.[16]

FURTHER RESOURCES

PERSONAL ACCOUNTS OF GRIEF

Abrams, R. (1992) *When Parents Die.* **London: Charles Letts & Co. Ltd.**
A refreshingly honest account of a teenage girl's grief in response to the death of her father (she was 18), followed two years later by the death of her stepfather. It also includes the findings from the author's interviews with many bereaved teenagers and young adults.

Abse, D. (2007) *The Presence.* **London: Hutchinson.**
A very moving, but also celebratory and humorous diary-based account of the poet's attempt to come to terms with the death of his wife of over 50 years in a car accident.

Cockburn, A. M. (2015) *5,742 Days: A Mother's Journey Through Loss.* **Oxford: Infinite Ideas Limited.**
A very moving, but also hopeful, account of a mother's attempt to live without her teenage daughter – and only child – following a drug 'accident'.

Lewis, C. S. (1961) *A Grief Observed.* **London: Faber & Faber.**
A classic account of the famous author's grief following the death of his beloved 'H'.

REFLECTIONS ON DEATH AND DYING

Bradley, R. (2016) *A Matter of Life and Death.* **London: Jessica Kingsley Publishers.**
Sixty people from all walks of life share their thoughts and feelings about carefully selected writings, images, and artwork which capture their idea of death. In all cases, understanding and 'welcoming' death is seen as crucial to how we live our lives.

Dinnage, R. (1990) *The Ruffian on the Stair: Reflections on Death.* **London: Penguin.**
A collection of fascinating and thought-provoking interviews with 24 people of diverse ages and backgrounds.

Keizer, B. (1997) *Dancing with Mister D: Notes on Life and Death.* **London: Black Swan.**
The extraordinary – and often darkly humorous – story of a doctor's work with both young and old terminally ill patients in a Dutch hospice.

Kübler-Ross, E. (1998) *The Wheel of Life: A Memoir of Living and Dying.* **London: Bantam.**
The author of the influential *On Death and Dying* (1969), which identifies five major stages of grief.

MORE ACADEMIC TEXTS

Bonanno, G. A. (2009) *The Other Side of Sadness.* **New York: Basic Books.**
An account of grief which challenges traditional beliefs regarding the inevitability of grief and sorrow: we're far more resilient in the face of loss, which can actually help us find new meaning in life.

Parkes, C. M. & Prigerson, H. G. (2010) *Bereavement: Studies of Grief in Adult Life* **(4th edition). London: Penguin Books.**
This is the latest edition of one of the classic British texts. It summarises recent research findings in an accessible way, making it suitable for both bereaved people and those trying to support them – both family and professionals.

POETRY

Astley, N. (2003) (ed.) *Do Not Go Gentle: Poems for Funerals.* **Tarset: Bloodaxe Books.**

Benson, J. & Falk, A. (1996) (eds.) *The Long Pale Corridor: Contemporary Poems of Bereavement*. Newcastle-upon-Tyne: Bloodaxe Books.

Paterson, D. (2012) (ed.) *The Picador Book of Funeral Poems*. London: Picador.

PSYCHOTHERAPISTS' ACCOUNTS OF PATIENTS' GRIEF/FEAR OF DEATH

Samuel, J. (2017) *Grief Works: Stories of Life, Death and Surviving*. London: Penguin Life.

Yalom, I. D. (2015) *Creatures of a Day: And Other Tales of Psychotherapy*. London: Piatkus.
While Samuel's book focuses more on bereavement and grief, Yalom is more concerned with how we face the inevitability of death and our responsibility for leading life worth living.

FILMS

Amour (France, 2012) This examines the close bond between an elderly French couple (Emmanuelle Riva and Jean-Louis Trintignant) as she becomes terminally ill. It presents a heart-rending story of sacrifice and devotion and the lengths that love can drive us to: pained by watching his beloved slowly fading away, he suffocates her as his final act of love.

Ghost (U.S., 1990) Sam (Patrick Swayze) and Molly (Demi Moore) are a young couple madly in love. Sam is murdered. The film explores her continuing relationship with the deceased Sam.

Ordinary People (U.S., 1980) The accidental death of the oldest son of an affluent American family puts a huge strain on the relationship between the bitter mother (Mary Tyler Moore), good-natured father, (Donald Sutherland), and guilt-ridden younger son/brother (Timothy Hutton).

Truly, Madly, Deeply (U.K., 1990) Nina (Juliet Stephenson) is devastated by the death of her boyfriend (Alan Rickman), who appears to her as a ghost – almost as if he were confused by her palpable grief.

USEFUL WEBSITES (MAINLY U.K.)

GENERAL

Age UK www.ageuk.org.uk

Bereavement UK www.bereavement.co.uk

British Association for Counselling and Psychotherapy (BACP) www.bacp.co.uk

Childhood Bereavement Network www.childhoodbereavementnetwork.org.uk

Cruse Bereavement Care www.crusebereavementcare.org.uk (A related site [for young people] is RD4U ['The road for you'] www.rd4u.org.uk.)

Dying Matters www.dyingmatters.org

Healthtalkonline www.healthtalkonline.org

Macmillan Cancer Support www.macmillan.org.uk

Merry Widow www.merrywidow.me.uk

MIND (The National Mental Health Charity) www.mind.org.uk

National Association of Bereavement Services www.self-help.org.uk

Samaritans www.samaritans.org.uk

WAY Widowed And YOUNG www. widowedandyoung.org

Westminster Pastoral Foundation www.wpf.org.uk

Women's Therapy Centre (WTC) www.womenstherapycentre.co.uk

LOSS OF A CHILD

The Child Bereavement Trust www.childbereavement.org.uk

The Compassionate Friends www.tcf.org.uk

Lullaby Trust http:/www.lullabytrust.org.uk

Grief Encounter www.griefencounter.com

Miscarriage Association www.miscarriageassociation.org.uk

Much Loved (online tribute charity) www.muchloved.com

Sands (Stillbirth and Neonatal Death Charity) www.uk-sands.org

Support in Bereavement for Brothers and Sisters (SIBBS) helpline: 08451 232304

Together for Short Lives www.togetherforshortlives.org.uk

CHILDREN AND TEENAGERS

Childline www.childline.org.uk

Siblinks www.siblinks.org

Teenage Cancer Trust www.teenagecancertrust.org

Winston's Wish www.winstonswish.org.uk

SUDDEN, VIOLENT, AND TRAUMATIC BEREAVEMENT

American Association of Suicidology (AAS) www.suicidology.org

American Foundation for Suicide Prevention (AFSD) www.afsp.org

BRAKE (The Road Safety Charity) www.brake.org.uk

Centre for Suicide Research (University of Oxford) www.psychiatry.ox.ac.uk/csr

The Compassionate Friends: Shadow of Suicide Group (SOS) www.tcf.org.uk

Homicide Victims' Support Group (Australia) Inc. hvsgnsw.org.au

Inquest www.inquest.org.uk

International Association for Suicide Prevention (IASP) www.iasp.info

National Association of Victim Support Schemes www.counselling-directory.org.uk

PAPYRUS www.papyrus-uk.org

Roadpeace www.roadpeace.org

Royal Society for the Prevention of Accidents (ROSPA) www.rospa.com

SAMM (Support after Murder and Manslaughter) www.samm.org.uk

SAMMA (Support after Murder and Manslaughter Abroad) www.sammabroad.org

SAVE (Suicide Awareness Voices of Education) – Coping with Loss www.save.org/coping

SCARD (Support and Care After Road Death) www.scard.org.uk

SOBS (Survivors of Bereavement by Suicide) www.uk-sobs.org.uk

Suicide Prevention Information New Zealand (SPINZ) www.spinz.org.nz

FAITH AND MINORITY GROUPS

Asian Family Counselling Service: Tel. Helpline 020 8571 3933

Interfaith Seminary www.theinterfaithseminary.com

In Truth One Spirit: Tel. Helpline 01483 898969

Islamic Cultural Centre www.iccuk.org

Jewish Bereavement Counselling Service www.jbcs.org.uk (London-based)

Lesbian and Gay Bereavement Project Tel. Helpline 0207 7403 5969

Muslim Women's Helpline: 020 8904 8193/020 8908 6715

Switchboard, the LGBT+ Helpline www.pinknews.co.uk

FUNERALS

British Humanist Association www.humanism.org.uk

Cremation Society of GB www.cremation.org.uk

National Association of Funeral Directors (NAFD) www.nafd.org.uk

Natural Death Centre www.naturaldeath.org.uk

NOTES

CHAPTER 1

1 Doka & Martin (2010)
2 Rando (1993)
3 Parkes (2006) (p. 166)
4 Raphael (1984) (p. 227)
5 Parkes (1971)
6 Raphael (1984) identifies 'delayed' and inhibited' grief; 'absent' (or 'minimal) and 'chronic' grief are used by Bowlby (1980).
7 Doka (1989); Doka (2002)
8 Doka & Martin (2010)
9 *Ibid.*
10 *Ibid.*
11 *Macbeth*, 4.3, lines 209–210
12 Doka & Martin (2010) (p. 60)
13 Freud (1917/1953)
14 Doka (1989)
15 A common distinction is made between (i) grief as the *internal* response to the death of a loved one and (ii) mourning as the *external* expression of grief. However, for clarity if nothing else, I prefer to use 'grief' for both (i) and (ii) and 'mourning' to denote the social rituals surrounding bereavement.
16 Abse (2007); Barnes (2013); Lewis (1961)

17 Parkes (1965a); Parkes (1965b)

18 Parkes (1970)

19 It is widely accepted that grief reactions will be heightened (or will reappear after the griever has largely adapted to the loss) on particular occasions following a bereavement. The 'anniversary reaction' refers to the anniversary of the death, but there can be a number of anniversaries and 'firsts' (such as first Christmas following the bereavement, the loved one's birthday, the couple's wedding anniversary, and so on) which can have the same effect.

20 Glick et al. (1974)

21 The purpose of the control (or *comparison*) group was to ensure that the only major – and relevant – difference between the two groups was that one had suffered bereavement and the other hadn't. This allowed the researchers to attribute any psychological/psychiatric differences between them to bereavement (rather than age differences, etc.)

22 Parkes (2006)

CHAPTER 2

1 'Theories' are, strictly, attempts to *explain* some phenomenon, rather than merely describe it. Despite this, stage or phase accounts, like those of Bowlby, Bowlby and Parkes, and Kübler-Ross, are commonly referred to as 'theories'.

2 Bowlby (1980); Bowlby & Parkes (1970)

3 Kübler-Ross (1969)

4 March & Doherty (1999)

5 Parkinson (1992)

6 Bowlby (1980)

7 Parkinson (1992)

8 Archer (1999)

9 Lewis (1961) (p. 49)

10 *Ibid.* (pp. 50–51)

11 Parkes (2013)

12 Robertson & Bowlby (1952)

13 Ramsay & de Groot (1977)

14 Barnes (2013)

15 Archer (1999)

16 Parkes & Prigerson (2010)

17 Maciejewski et al. (2007)

18 Parkes & Prigerson (2010)

19 Prigerson & Maciejewski (2008)

20 Lakoff & Johnson (1980)

21 Nadeau (2008)

22 Corless et al. (2014)

23 Cockburn (2015)

24 Lewis (1961) (p. 5)

25 Dixey (2016) (p. 92)

26 Hirsch (2014) *Gabriel*

27 Froggatt (1998)

28 Moules, Simonson, Prins et al. (2004)

29 Nadeau (2008)

30 Tonkin (1996)

31 Graves (2009) (p. 147)

32 *Ibid.*

33 Abse (2007) (p. 13)

34 *Ibid.* (p. 106)

35 Weiss (1993)

36 Wortman & Silver (1989)

37 Wortman & Boerner (2011)

38 Bonnano (2009)

39 *Ibid.* (p. 7–8)

40 *Ibid.*

41 *Ibid.*

42 Kastenbaum (2008)

CHAPTER 3

1 Parkes (2006) (p. 1)

2 According to Lorenz, goslings and ducklings learn to follow the first moving object they see after hatching. They become 'imprinted' on this object (usually the mother, but, famously, Lorenz himself), which keeps them safe and provides them with food.

3 Baby rhesus monkeys removed from their mothers and raised with just surrogate (substitutes made from wire) mothers, preferred one covered in soft terry cloth to one without cloth but which provided milk.

4 Fletcher (2002) (p. 89)

5   Shaver et al. (1996)

6   Shaver & Fraley (2008)

7   Ainsworth et al. (1978)

8   Main (1991)

9   Hazan & Shaver (1987)

10 Parkes (2006)

11 Freud (1912–13/1961) (p. 65)

12 Stroebe & Schut (1999)

13 Stroebe (1992)

14 Lindemann (1944)

15 Bowlby (1979)

16 Stroebe & Schut (1999)

17 Stroebe (1992)

18 Wortman & Silver (1987)

19 Stroebe & Schut (2010)

20 Worden (2009) (Note the use of 'mourning' in the title, reflecting Freud's use of the term, rather than the more usual 'grieving'; see Chapter 1.)

21 Gorer (1965)

22 Corr & Corr (2013)

23 Parkes (1993)

24 *Ibid.* (p. 94)

25 *Ibid.* (p. 95)

26 Parkes (2006)

27 Stroebe & Schut (1999)

28 Stroebe & Schut (2010)

29 Zech & Arnold (2011)

30 Stroebe et al. (2005)

31 Ogden et al. (2006)

32 Stroebe & Schut (2010)

33 Wikan (1988)

34 An account of grief that is complementary to the DPM is Rubin's (1999) two-track model (TTM). (See Gross, 2016).

35 Fraley & Shaver (1999)

36 In fact, even Freud himself, at least in his personal correspondence, did not agree with the extreme position that later writers attributed to him (Shaver & Fraley, 2008).

37 Stroebe & Schut (2005)

38 Lewis (1961) (p. 6)

39 Field (2006)
40 Bowlby (1980) (p. 100)
41 Yo et al. (2013)

CHAPTER 4

1 Prior (1989)
2 Lindemann (1944)
3 Engel (1961)
4 Prior (1989)
5 As in, for example, Freud's stages of psychosexual development, Erikson's stages of psychosocial development, and Piaget's stages of cognitive development: see Gross (2015)
6 Cited in Prior (1989)
7 Ibid.
8 Radcliffe-Brown (1922)
9 Prior (1989) (p. 109)
10 Gorer (1965) (p. 113)
11 Walter (1993)
12 Ibid.
13 Aries (1981)
14 Walter (1993)
15 Becker (1973)
16 Clark (1993)
17 Cook (2013)
18 Ibid.
19 Ibid.
20 Ibid.
21 Ibid.
22 Parkes & Prigerson (2010)
23 Ibid. (p. 205)
24 Ibid.
25 Nichols & Nichols (1975)
26 Orbach (1999)
27 Holloway et al. (2013)
28 Ibid.
29 Holloway et al. (2011)
30 Ibid.
31 Ibid.

32 Attig (2004)

33 Doka (2002)

34 Shapiro (2013)

35 Klass & Chow (2011)

36 Rosenblatt (1975)

37 Klass & Chow (2011)

38 Ibid.

39 Ibid.

40 Neimeyer (2001)

41 Walter (1999)

42 Klass & Chow (2011)

43 Kleinman & Kleinman (1985)

44 Klass & Chow (2011)

CHAPTER 5

1 Carr & Jeffreys (2011)

2 Bennett & Soulsby (2012)

3 Ibid.

4 Parkes (2006)

5 Ibid.

6 Parkes (2006) (p. 158)

7 Debbie Kerslake, Cruse Chief Executive, personal communication.

8 Parkes (2006)

9 Abrams (1992)

10 Ibid. (p xiii)

11 Balk (2013)

12 Moss et al. (2001)

13 Parkes (2006)

14 Ibid.

15 Ibid. (p. 160)

16 Dunn (2000)

17 Marshall & Davies (2011)

18 Ibid.

19 Rowe (2007)

20 Connidis (1992)

21 Rowe (2007)

22 Raphael (1984) (p. 227)

23 Parkes (2006) (p. 166)

24 This can be accounted for by *evolutionary theory* (see Gross, 2016)

25 Parkes (2006)

26 Raphael (1984)

27 *Ibid.*

28 Buggins (1995)

29 Balk (2013)

30 Raphael (1984)

31 *Ibid.*

32 Prigerson & Jacobs (2001)

33 Umphrey & Cacciotore (2014)

34 *Ibid.*

35 Buckle & Fleming (2011)

36 *Ibid.* (p. 93)

CHAPTER 6

1 Freud (1917/1953)

2 Bowlby (1980)

3 Kübler-Ross (1969)

4 Worden (1982)

5 Stroebe & Schut (1999, 2010)

6 Parkes (1972)

7 Klass et al. (1999)

8 Bonnano (2009)

9 Currier et al. (2008)

10 Klass et al. (1999)

11 Carr (2010)

12 Stroebe & Schut (2010)

13 Zech & Arnold (2011)

14 *Ibid.*

15 Stroebe et al. (2005)

16 Neimeyer (2011)

17 Jordan & McIntosh (2011)

18 Keesee et al. (2008)

19 Neimeyer & Jordan (2013)

20 Stroebe et al. (2013)

21 Parkes & Prigerson (2010)

22 *Ibid.*

23 Neimeyer & Jordan (2013)

24 Rando (2013)

25 Parkes & Prigerson (2010)

26 Burke & Neimeyer (2013)

27 Rosenblatt (2013)

28 *Ibid.*

29 Parkes & Prigerson (2010)

30 Parkes & Weiss (1983)

31 Raphael (1984)

32 Parkes & Prigerson (2010)

33 Jordan & McIntosh (2011)

34 *Ibid.*

35 Pitman et al. (2014)

36 Jordan & McIntosh (2011) (p. 227)

37 Payne et al. (2008)

CHAPTER 7

1 Neimeyer & Sands (2011) (p. 9) (emphasis in original)

2 *Ibid.* (p. 10)

3 *Ibid.*

4 Neimeyer (2006)

5 Neimeyer & Sands (2011)

6 Attig (2000)

7 Prigerson et al. (2009)

8 Keesee et al. (2008)

9 Linley & Joseph (2003)

10 Tedeschi & Calhoun (1996)

11 Seligman (2011)

12 Calhoun & Tedeschi (1999)

13 Linley & Joseph (2004)

14 Calhoun et al. (2010)

15 Joseph (2012)

16 *Ibid.* (p. 817)

REFERENCES

Abrams, R. (1992) *When Parents Die*. London: Charles Letts & Co.

Abse, D. (2007) *The Presence*. London: Hutchinson.

Ainsworth, M. D. S., Blehar, N. C., Waters, E. & Wall, S. (1978) *Patterns of Attachment: A Psychological Study of the Strange Situation*. Hillsdale, NJ: Lawrence Erlbaum Associates.

American Psychiatric Association (2000) *Diagnostic and Statistical Manual of Mental Disorders* (4th edition revised). Washington, DC: American Psychiatric Association.

Archer, J. (1999) *The Nature of Grief: The Evolution and Psychology of Reactions to Loss*. London: Routledge.

Aries, P. (1981) *The Hour of Our Death*. London: Allen Lane.

Attig, T. (2000) *The Heart of Grief*. New York: Oxford University Press.

Attig, T. (2004) Disenfranchised grief revisited: Discounting hope and love. *Omega*, 49(3), 197–215.

Balk, D. E. (2013) Life span issues and loss, grief and mourning: Adulthood. In D. K. Meagher & D. E. Balk (eds.) *Handbook of Thanatology: The Essential Body of Knowledge for the Study of Death, Dying and Bereavement* (2nd edition). New York: Routledge.

Barnes, J. (2013) *Levels of Life*. London: Jonathan Cape.

Becker, E. (1973) *The Denial of Death*. New York: Free Press.

Bennett, K. M. & Soulsby, L. K. (2012) Wellbeing in bereavement and widowhood. *Illness, Crisis & Loss*, 20(4), 321–337.

Bonnano, G. A. (2009) *The Other Side of Sadness: What the New Science of Bereavement Tells Us About Life After Loss*. New York: Basic Books.

Bowlby, J. (1979) The making and breaking of affectional bonds. In J. Bowlby (ed.) *The Making and Breaking of Affectional Bonds*. London: Tavistock.

Bowlby, J. (1980) *Attachment and Loss, Vol. 3: Loss, Sadness, and Depression*. London: Hogarth Press.

Bowlby, J. & Parkes, C. M. (1970) Separation and loss within the family. In E. J. Anthony (ed.) *The Child in His Family*. New York: Wiley.

Buckle, J. L. & Fleming, S. J. (2011) Parenting challenges after the death of a child. In R. A. Neimeyer et al. (eds.) *Grief and Bereavement in Contemporary Society: Bridging Research and Practice*. New York: Routledge.

Buggins, E. (1995) Mind your language. *Nursing Standard*, 10(1), 21–22.

Burke, L. A. & Neimeyer, R. A. (2013) Prospective risk factors for complicated grief: A review of the empirical literature. In M. Stroebe et al. (eds.) *Complicated Grief: Scientific Foundations for Health Care Professionals*. London: Routledge.

Calhoun, L. G., Cann, A. & Tedeschi, R. G. (2010) The posttraumatic growth model: Socio-cultural considerations. In T. Weiss & R. Berger (eds.) *Posttraumatic Growth and Culturally Competent Practice: Lessons Learned from Around the Globe*. New York: Wiley.

Calhoun, L. G. & Tedeschi, R. G. (1999) *Facilitating Posttraumatic Growth: A Clinician's Guide*. Mahwah, NJ: Lawrence Relbaum.

Carr, D. (2010) New perspectives on the dual process model (DPM): What have we learned? What questions remain? *Omega: Journal of Death & Dying*, 63, 371–380.

Carr, D. & Jeffreys, J. S. (2011) Spousal bereavement in later life. In R. A. Neimeyer et al. (eds.) *Grief and Bereavement in Contemporary Society: Bridging Research and Practice*. New York: Routledge.

Clark, D. (1993) Death in Staithes. In D. Dickenson & M. Johnson (eds.) *Death, Dying and Bereavement*. London: Sage Publications and the Open University. (Abridged extract from *Between Pulpit and Pew* (1982) Cambridge: Cambridge University Press.)

Cockburn, A. M. (2015) *5,742 Days: A Mother's Journey Through Loss*. Oxford: Infinite Ideas Limited.

Connidis, I. A. (1992) Life transitions and the adult sibling tie: A qualitative study. *Journal of Marriage & The Family*, 54(4), 972–982.

Cook, A. S. (2013) The family, larger systems, and loss, grief and mourning. In D. K. Meagher & D. E. Balk (eds.) *Handbook of Thanatology: The Essential Body of Knowledge for the Study of Death, Dying and Bereavement* (2nd edition). New York: Routledge.

Corless, B., Limbo, R., Bousso, R. S. et al. (2014) Language of grief: A model for understanding the expressions of the bereaved. *Health Psychology & Behavioural Medicine*, 2(1), 132–143.

Corr, C. A. & Corr, D. M. (2013) Culture, socialisation, and dying. In D. K. Meagher & D. E. Balk (eds.) *Handbook of Thanatology: The Essential Body of Knowledge for the Study of Death, Dying and Bereavement* (2nd edition). New York: Routledge.

Currier, J. M., Neimeyer, R. A. & Berman, J. S. (2008) The effectiveness of psychotherapeutic interventions for the bereaved: A comprehensive qualitative study. *Psychological Bulletin*, 134, 648–661.

Dixey, R. (2016) Wish me luck as you wave me goodbye. *Bereavement Care*, 35(3), 92–93.

Doka, K. J. (1989) *Disenfranchised Grief: Recognising Hidden Sorrow*. San Francisco, CA: Jossey-Bass.

Doka, K. J. (2002) *Disenfranchised Grief: New Directions, Challenges and Strategies for Practice*. Champaign, IL: Research Press.

Doka, K. J. & Martin, T. L. (2010) *Grieving Beyond Gender: Understanding the Ways Men and Women Mourn* (revised edition). New York: Routledge.

Dunn, J. (2000) Siblings. *The Psychologist*, 13(5), 244–248. (p. 244).

Engel, G. (1961) Is grief a disease? *Psychosomatic Medicine*, 23, 18–22.

Field, N. P. (2006) Unresolved grief and Continuing Bonds: An attachment perspective. *Death Studies*, 30, 739–756.

Fletcher, G. (2002) *The New Science of Intimate Relationships*. Oxford: Blackwell.

Fraley, R. C. & Shaver, P. R. (1999) Loss and bereavement: Bowlby's theory and recent controversies concerning grief work and the nature of detachment. In J. Cassidy & P. R. Shaver (eds.) *Handbook of Attachment: Theory, Research and Clinical Applications*. New York: Guilford Press.

Freud, S. (1912–13/1961) *Totem and Taboo: Standard Edition of the Complete Psychological Works of Sigmund Freud*, Vol. 13. London: Hogarth Press.

Freud, S. (1917/1953) *Mourning and Melancholia: Standard Edition of the Complete Psychological Works of Sigmund Freud*, Vol. 14. London: Hogarth Press.

Froggatt, K. (1998) The place of metaphor and language in exploring nurses' emotional work. *Journal of Advanced Nursing*, 28(2), 332–338.

Glick, I., Parkes, C. M. & Weiss, R. S. (1974) *The First Year of Bereavement*. Chichester: Wiley Interscience.

Gorer, G. (1965) *Death, Grief, and Mourning in Contemporary Britain*. London: Cresset.

Graves, J. (2009) *Talking with Bereaved People: An Approach for Structured and Sensitive Communication*. London: Jessica Kingsley Publishers.

Gross, R. (2015) *Psychology: The Science of Mind and Behaviour* (7th edition). London: Hodder Education.

Gross, R. (2016) *Understanding Grief: An Introduction*. London: Routledge.

Hazan, C. & Shaver, P. R. (1987) Romantic love conceptualised as an attachment process. *Journal of Personality & Social Psychology*, 52(3), 511–524.

Hirsch, E. (2014) *Gabriel: A Poem*. New York: Knopf Publishing Group.

Holloway, M., Adamson, S., Argyrou, V. et al. (2013) 'Funerals aren't nice but it couldn't have been nicer': The makings of a good funeral. *Mortality*, 18(1), 30–53.

Holloway, M., Adamson, S., McSherry, W. & Swinton, J. (2011) *Spiritual Care at the End of Life: A Systematic Review of the Literature*. Retrieved from www.dh.gov.uk/publications

Jordan, J. R. & McIntosh, J. L. (2011) Is suicide bereavement different? Perspectives from research and practice. In R. A. Neimeyer et al. (eds.) *Grief and Bereavement in Contemporary Society: Bridging Research and Practice*. New York: Routledge.

Joseph, S. (2012) What doesn't kill us . . . *Psychologist*, 25(11), 816–819.

Kastenbaum, R. (2008) Grieving in contemporary society. In M. S. Stroebe, R. O. Hansson, H. Schut & W. Stroebe (eds.) *Handbook of Bereavement Research and Practice: Advances in Theory and Intervention*. Washington, DC: American Psychological Association.

Keesee, N. J., Currier, J. M. & Neimeyer, R. A. (2008) Predictors of grief following the death of one's child: The contribution of finding meaning. *Journal of Clinical Psychology*, 64, 1145–1163.

Klass, D. & Chow, A. Y. M. (2011) Culture and ethnicity in experiencing, policing and handling grief. In R. A. Neimeyer et al. (eds.) *Grief and Bereavement in Contemporary Society: Bridging Research and Practice*. New York: Routledge.

Klass, D., Siverman, P. R. & Nickman, S. (1999) (eds.) *Continuing Bonds: New Understandings of Grief*. Washington, DC: Taylor & Francis.

Kleinman, A. & Kleinman, J. (1985) Somatisation: The interconnections in Chinese society among culture, depressive experiences, and the meanings of pain. In A. Kleinman & B. Good (eds.) *Culture and Depression: Studies in the Anthropology and Cross-Cultural Psychology of Affect and Disorder*. Berkeley, CA: University of California Press.

Kübler-Ross, E. (1969) *On Death and Dying*. London: Tavistock/Routledge.

Lakoff, G. & Johnson, M. (1980) (New Afterword, 2003) *Metaphors We Live By*. Chicago: University of Chicago Press.

Lewis, C. S. (1961) *A Grief Observed*. London: Faber & Faber.

Lindemann, E. (1944) The symptomatology and management of acute grief. *American Journal of Psychiatry*, 101, 155–160.

Linley, P. A. & Joseph, S. (2003) Trauma and personal growth. *Psychologist*, 16(3), 135.

Linley, P. A. & Joseph, S. (2004) Positive change processes following trauma and adversity: A review of the empirical literature. *Journal of Traumatic Stress*, 17, 11–22.

Maciejewski, P. K., Zhang, B., Block, S. D. & Prigerson, H. G. (2007) An empirical investigation of the stage theory of grief. *Journal of the American Medical Association*, 297(7), 716–723.

Main, M. (1991) Metacognitive knowledge, metacognitive monitoring, and singular (coherent) versus multiple (incoherent) models of attachment: Findings and directions for future research. In C. M. Parkes, J. M. Stephenson-Hinde & P. Marris (eds.) *Attachment Across the Life Cycle*. London: Routledge.

March, P. & Doherty, C. (1999) Dying and bereavement. In D. Messer & F. Jones (eds.) *Psychology and Social Care*. London: Jessica Kingsley Publishers.

Marshall, B. & Davies, B. (2011) Bereavement in children and adults following the death of a sibling. In R. A. Neimeyer et al. (eds.) *Grief and Bereavement in Contemporary Society: Bridging Research and Practice*. New York: Routledge.

Moss, M. S., Moss, S. Z. & Hansson, R. (2001) Bereavement in old age. In M. Stroebe et al. (eds.) *Handbook of Bereavement Research: Consequences, Coping and Care*. Washington, DC: American Psychological Association.

Moules, N. J., Simonson, K., Prins, M. et al. (2004) Making room for grief: Walking backwards and living forward. *Nursing Inquiry*, 11(2), 99–107.

Nadeau, J. W. (2008) Meaning-making in bereaved families: Assessment, intervention and future research. In M. S. Stroebe, R. O. Hansson, H. Schut & W. Stroebe (eds.) *Handbook of Bereavement Research and Practice: Advances in Theory and Intervention*. Washington, DC: American Psychological Association.

Neimeyer, R. A. (2001) Meaning reconstruction and loss. In R. A. Neimeyer (ed.) *Meaning Reconstructions and the Experience of Loss.* Washington, DC: American Psychological Association.

Neimeyer, R. A. (2006) Complicated grief and the quest for meaning: A constructivist contribution. *Journal of Death & Dying,* 52, 37–52.

Neimeyer, R. A. (2011) Reconstructing meaning in bereavement. In W. Watson & D. Kissane (eds.) *Handbook of Psychotherapies in Cancer Care.* New York: Wiley.

Neimeyer, R. A. & Jordan, J. R. (2013) Historical and contemporary perspectives on assessment and intervention. In D. K. Meagher & D. E. Balk (eds.) *Handbook of Thanatology: The Essential Body of Knowledge for the Study of Death, Dying and Bereavement* (2nd edition). New York: Routledge.

Neimeyer, R. A. & Sands, D. C. (2011) Meaning reconstruction in bereavement: From principles to practice. In R. A. Neimeyer, D. L. Harris, H. R. Winokuer & G. F. Thornton (eds.) *Grief and Bereavement in Contemporary Society: Bridging Research and Practice.* New York: Routledge.

Nichols, R. & Nichols, J. (1975) Funerals: A time for grief and growth. In E. Kübler-Ross (ed.) *Death: The Final Stage of Growth.* Englewood Cliffs, NJ: Prentice Hall.

Ogden, P., Minton, K. & Pain, C. (2006) *Trauma and the Body: A Sensorimotor Approach to Psychotherapy.* New York: Norton.

Orbach, A. (1999) *Life, Psychotherapy, and Death: The End of Our Exploring.* London: Jessica Kingsley Publishers.

Parkes, C. M. (1965a) Bereavement and mental illness: Part 1. A clinical study of the grief of bereaved psychiatric patients. *British Journal of Medical Psychology,* 38, 1–12.

Parkes, C. M. (1965b) Bereavement and mental illness: Part 2. A classification of bereavement reactions. *British Journal of Medical Psychology,* 38, 13–26.

Parkes, C. M. (1970) The first year of bereavement: A longitudinal study of the reaction of London widows to the death of their husbands. *Psychiatry,* 33, 444–467.

Parkes, C. M. (1971) Psychosocial transitions: A field for study. *Social Science & Medicine,* 5, 101–115.

Parkes, C. M. (1972) *Bereavement: Studies of Grief in Adult Life.* London: Tavistock Publications.

Parkes, C. M. (1993) Bereavement as a psychosocial transition: Processes of adaptation to change. In M. S. Stroebe, W. Stroebe & R. O. Hansson (eds.)

Handbook of Bereavement: Theory, Research and Intervention. New York: Cambridge University Press.

Parkes, C. M. (2006) *Love and Loss: The Roots of Grief and Its Complications.* London: Routledge.

Parkes, C. M. (2013) Elizabeth Kübler-Ross, On Death and Dying: A Reappraisal. *Mortality: Promoting the Interdisciplinary Study of Death and Dying,* 18(1), 94–97.

Parkes, C. M. & Prigerson, H. G. (2010) *Bereavement: Studies of Grief in Adult Life* (4th edition). London: Penguin Books.

Parkes, C. M. & Weiss, R. S. (1983) *Recovery from Bereavement.* New York: Basic Books.

Parkinson, P. (1992) Coping with dying and bereavement. *Nursing Standard,* 6(17), 36–38.

Payne, S., Swami, V. & Stanistreet, D. (2008) The social construction of gender and its impact on suicidal behaviour. *Journal of Men's Health & Gender,* 5(1), 23–35.

Pitman, A., Osborn, D. P. J., King, M. B. & Erlangsen, A. (2014) Effects of suicide bereavement on mental health and suicide risk. *Lancet Psychiatry,* 1(1), 86–94.

Prigerson, H. G., Horowitz, M. J., Jacobs, S. C. et al. (2009) Prolonged grief disorder: Psychometric validation of criteria proposed for DSM-V and ICD-11. *PLoS Medicine,* 6(8), E1000121.

Prigerson, H. G. & Jacobs, S. C. (2001) Traumatic grief as a distinct disorder: A rationale, consensus criteria, and preliminary empirical test. In M. Stroebe et al. (eds.) *Handbook of Bereavement Research: Consequences, Coping and Care.* Washington, DC: American Psychological Association.

Prigerson, H. G. & Maciejewski, P. K. (2008) Grief and acceptance as opposite sides of the same coin: Setting a research agenda for studying peaceful acceptance of loss. *British Journal of Psychiatry,* 193, 435–437.

Prior, L. (1989) *The Social Organization of Death.* London: Macmillan.

Radcliffe-Brown, A. R. (1922) *The Andaman Islanders.* Cambridge: Cambridge University Press.

Ramsay, R. & de Groot, W. (1977) A further look at bereavement. Paper presented at EATI conference, Uppsala. Cited in P.E. Hodgkinson (1980) Treating abnormal grief in the bereaved. *Nursing Times,* 17 January, 126–128.

Rando, T. (1993) *Treatment of Complicated Mourning.* Champaign, IL: Research Press.

Rando, T. (2013) On achieving clarity regarding complicated grief: Lessons from clinical practice. In M. Stroebe et al. (eds.) *Complicated Grief: Scientific Foundations for Health Care Professionals.* London: Routledge.

Raphael, B. (1984) *The Anatomy of Bereavement: A Handbook for the Caring Professions*. London: Hutchinson.

Robertson, J. & Bowlby, J. (1952) Responses of young children to separation from their mothers. *Courier of the International Children's Centre*, Paris, II, 131–140.

Rosenblatt, P. C. (1975) Use of ethnography in understanding grief and mourning. In B. Schoenberg et al. (eds.) *Bereavement: Its Psychosocial Aspects*. New York: Columbia University Press.

Rosenblatt, P. C. (2013) Culture and socialisation in death, grief, and mourning. In M. Stroebe et al. (eds.) *Complicated Grief: Scientific Foundations for Health Care Professionals*. London: Routledge.

Rowe, D. (2007) *My Dearest Enemy, My Dangerous Friend: Making and Breaking Sibling Bonds*. Hove: Routledge.

Rubin, S. (1999) The two-track model of bereavement: Overview, retrospect and prospect. *Death Studies*, 23, 681–714.

Seligman, M.E.P. (2011) *Flourish*. New York: Free Press.

Shapiro, E. R. (2013) Culture and socialization in assessment and intervention. In D. K. Meagher & D. E. Balk (eds.) *Handbook of Thanatology: The Essential Body of Knowledge for the Study of Death, Dying and Bereavement* (2nd edition). New York: Routledge.

Shaver, P. R., Collins, N. & Clark, C. L. (1996) Attachment styles and internal working models of self and relationship patterns. In G. J. O. Fletcher & J. Fitness (eds.) *Knowledge Structure in Close Relationships: A Social Psychological Approach*. Mahwah, NJ: Lawrence Erlbaum Associates.

Shaver, P. R. & Fraley, C. (2008) Attachment, loss and grief: Bowlby's views and current controversies. In J. Cassidy & P. R. Shaver (eds.) *Handbook of Attachment* (2nd edition). New York: Guilford Press.

Stroebe, M. (1992) Coping with bereavement: A review of the grief work hypothesis. *Omega*, 26, 19–42.

Stroebe, M., Hansson, R. O., Schut, H. and Stroebe, W. (2008) (eds.) *Handbook of Bereavement Research and Practice: Advances in Theory and Intervention*. Washington, DC: American Psychological Association.

Stroebe, M. & Schut, H. (1999) The dual process model of coping with bereavement: Rationale and description. *Death Studies*, 23, 197–224.

Stroebe, M. & Schut, H. (2010) The dual process model of coping with bereavement: Rationale and description. *Omega*, 61(4), 273–289.

Stroebe, M., Schut, H. & van den Bout, J. (2013) (eds.) Introduction. In *Complicated Grief: Scientific Foundations for Health Care Professionals*. London: Routledge.

Stroebe, W. & Schut, H. (2005) To continue or relinquish bonds: A review of consequences for the bereaved. *Death Studies*, 29, 477–494.

Stroebe, W., Schut, H. & Stroebe, M. (2005) Grief work, disclosure and counselling: Do they help the bereaved? *Clinical Psychology Review*, 25, 395–414.

Tedeschi, R. G. & Calhoun, L. G. (1996) The posttraumatic growth inventory: Measuring the positive legacy of trauma. *Journal of Traumatic Stress*, 9, 455–471.

Tonkin, L. (1996) Growing around grief: Another way of looking at grief and recovery. *Bereavement Care*, 15(11), 10.

Umphrey, L. R. & Cacciotore, J. (2014) Love and death: Relational metaphors following the death of a child. *Journal of Relationships Research*, 5, e4, 1–8.

Walter, T. (1993) Modern death: Taboo or not taboo? *Sociology*, 25(2), 293–310.

Walter, T. (1999) *On Bereavement: The Culture of Grief*. Buckingham: Open University Press.

Weiss, R. (1993) Loss and recovery. In M. Stroebe, W. Stroebe & R. O. Hansson (eds.) *Handbook of Bereavement: Theory, Research and Intervention*. New York: Cambridge University Press.

Wikan, U. (1988) Bereavement and loss in two Muslim communities: Egypt and Bali compared. *Social Science & Medicine*, 27, 451–460.

Worden, J. W. (1982) *Grief Counselling and Grief Therapy: A Handbook for the Mental Health Practitioner*. New York: Springer.

Worden, J. W. (2009) *Grief Counselling and Grief Therapy: A Handbook for the Mental Health Practitioner* (4th edition). New York: Springer.

Wortman, C. B. & Boerner, K. (2011) Beyond the myths of coping with loss: Prevailing assumptions versus scientific evidence. In H. S Friedman (ed.) *Oxford Handbook of Health Psychology*. New York: Oxford University Press.

Wortman, C. B. & Silver, R. C. (1987) Coping with irrevocable loss. In G. R. Vanden Bos & B. K. Bryant (eds.) *Cataclysms, Crises and Catastrophes: Psychology in Action*. Washington, DC: American Psychological Association.

Wortman, C. B. & Silver, R. C. (1989) The myth of coping with loss. *Journal of Consulting & Clinical Psychology*, 57, 349–357.

Yo, S. M. Y., Chan, I. S. F., Ma, E. P. W. & Field, N. P. (2013) Continuing Bonds, attachment style, and adjustment in the conjugal bereavement among Hong Kong Chinese. *Death Studies*, 37, 248–268.

Zech, E. & Arnold, C. (2011) Attachment and coping with bereavement: Implications for therapeutic interventions with the insecurely attached. In R. A. Neimeyer, D. L. Harris, H. R. Winokuer & G. F. Thornton (eds.) *Grief and Bereavement in Contemporary Society: Bridging Research and Practice*. New York: Routledge.

Printed in the United States
by Baker & Taylor Publisher Services